SPIRITUAL
TORRENTS

SPIRITUAL
TORRENTS

by

Jeanne Guyon

Spiritual Torrents

by

Jeanne Guyon

Copyright by Gene Edwards

MCMLXXXX

Published by
The SeedSowers
Christian Books Publishing House

ISBN 0-940232-18-9

ACKNOWLEDGEMENT

Acknowledgement must be given to Rose-Marie Slosek, who carried this book through three complete rewrites and to Denise Sirois, who typed the final drafts and to all the Christians who, through the years, have persistently asked that this book be published in modern English.

PREFACE

We had a bit of a problem bringing this particular book into modern English. There is a word which does not exist in the English language that *should* exist, a word which could mean either "he" or "she." In dealing with *Spiritual Torrents*, we very much missed this word. English should have a word like "s-he" or "sh-he" or something similar.

In this revision we were working with an Old English text which spoke constantly of "the soul . . . it!" Often "it" would appear twenty or more times on one page. The mind simply cannot follow a thought very long with so many pronouns in so short a space.

For "soul" we substituted the words "devotee," "believer," or "Christian"—in those places where no damage would be done to the original meaning. But there comes a time when you must decide to use "he" or "she"—the Christian "he" or "she." Poor English, our language cannot say" he-she" or "she-he"; therefore, we are bound to get into trouble with one of our two genders, once we make the choice. We did what writers and editors and translators have done for a thousand years in the presence of this language inadequacy— we elected to say the Christian "he," a choice which is only slightly better than the Christian "it." We apologize to all our female readers for this slighting, knowing full well it is the English language which should apologize.

One last thing. From time to time we are asked where we get copies of the original books we modernize, with an inevitable following question, "How can I get a copy?" The mystery is great. You do exactly what we do. Go to your public library and check the books out on an interlibrary loan! The librarian will explain the details.

And now, dear reader, to *Spiritual Torrents*, and a woman who did not flinch at telling of suffering the way it really is.

INTRODUCTION

The key to understanding this book is to see that it is Jeanne Guyon's own spiritual biography. She is the "torrent" in this book, and this is her story of her journey into Christ. This is *not* a book that tells you about the steps you need to go through in order to mature in Christ. To try to fit this book into your own life is to court disaster. Guyon wrote in another age, when it was necessary to describe everything in steps or stages. Further, she was very subjective, and perhaps even melancholy at times. What she speaks of in *Spiritual Torrents* really cannot be found in the New Testament . . . not as the way to know Christ. This is simply one woman's story, as she saw it in her life, as to what God did in dealing with her. The great strength of this book is simply this: There are very, very few books written on the subject of *the cross* as it relates to a Christian's walk. This is one of those few books. And it is a radical statement, even an extreme statement, about the way of the cross in the life of a believer.

Madame Guyon personally got into a lot of trouble from this book. Here is the story as best I can put it together.

Jeanne Guyon wrote her autobiography, commencing it in her thirties. But her first published book was the monumental work, *Method of Prayer,* now titled *Experiencing the Depths of Jesus Christ.* This is a masterpiece and a classic.

Her first imprisonment (actually it was *confinement* in a nunnery in a section of Paris called St. Anthony's) was caused by four factors: her half brother's plot to take her property and wealth from her . . . and the *three* books she had written up until then.

She was released by efforts of friends within the royal court of Louis XIV. After her release she entered into a period of her greatest popularity and influence—at Versaille, no less, the court of the most powerful monarch in all European history.

Guyon eventually fell into disfavor in Louis' court. The King personally asked that Bishop Bossuet, France's greatest and most famous churchman, *examine* her. This "examination" turned out to be a mental inquisition. Bossuet, the mightiest mind in France, thought he was dealing with a silly woman. He meant to steamroll her. Instead, he met his equal, if not his better. He was enraged. (History, of late, has not been kind to Bossuet, mostly because of his inordinate treatment of this woman.) Bossuet's conclusions about this "dangerous" woman caused Louis XIV to imprison Jeanne Guyon without *trial* or *charges.*

At her "hearing" before Bossuet and two other Bishops, Jeanne Guyon presented her autobiography to Bossuet. (He had already read *Method of Prayer* and was quite opposed to it.) She presented three other works to him at that time. Her choice could not have been worse. Out of her commentary on the Bible she chose her work on the *Song of Songs.* She also presented to him a recently completed manuscript of an unpublished book entitled *Spiritual Torrents.*

Imagine an overly pompous, overly pious single man in later life reading Guyon's intimate, passionate interpretation of *Song of Songs.* Bossuet's hair stood on end! Sex, after all, was a world unknown to him and certainly had no place in a religious book, even if it was on *Song of Songs.*

His reaction to *Spiritual Torrents* was worse. In this book Jeanne Guyon makes a left-hand attack on intellectualism and intellectuals . . . and that is about all Bossuet was! Furthermore, *Spiritual Torrents'* subjectivity did not appeal to one of the most objective minds France ever produced.

Another event, in another nation, also profoundly influenced what happened to Jeanne Guyon. Over in Italy a man named Michael Molinos was, at that very moment, imprisoned for similar writings.

Molinos had just recently turned Italy upside down, causing one of the biggest commotions ever to hit the Vatican, the Pope and Rome.

The teachings of these two people were not original with either, but had been taught in centuries past by canonized saints of the Catholic Church. It would never have entered the mind of Molinos or Guyon that what they wrote or taught could get them in trouble. It did.

Molinos was sealed in a dungeon. Guyon would very shortly find herself a fugitive from justice. When finally found, she was imprisoned in Vincennes, then in the infamous Bastille.

Guyon says an advanced stage of spirituality is rarely achieved. Something known to only a few, and even then, a state reached—usually—only in old age, only shortly before death. Well, she was in her late forties when she wrote this book. I assume, therefore, she herself was theorizing on some parts of what she wrote herein.

As far as I can discern, *Spiritual Torrents* was not published until after her death. One thing is certain: Whenever this book gets reprinted it always disturbs, upsets and confounds a lot of people.

Why, then, this new edition?

As stated earlier, there simply are not many pieces of Christian literature on the subject of the inwrought cross in the daily life of the believer. And the church today seems to be moving farther and farther from the subject of suffering . . . almost by the hour.

Most Christians, in reading this book, simply throw up their hands in dismay and try to forget they ever read it. That may very well be the most healthy thing you can do with it, *if* you believe that all Christians must go through the stages she describes. But, in fact, she is not saying that. To understand this particular book you must understand the Catholic tradition. Guyon may have been the most evangelical Roman Catholic to write a book in her time, but Catholic she was.

Now a Catholic who wrote on the subject which she wrote on here, in order to be considered a good Catholic, would have to follow a long and well-established tradition. This tradition was established back in the days of Augustine and Dionysius Exiguus. These two men put the Christian life in "stages." Every writer thereafter was bound by tradition to establish a set of stages through which he believed the soul must pass in order to arrive at "perfection." Perfection, to the Catholic mind, means neither sinlessness nor perfection . . . but a state of "being in God."

Guyon's purpose in this book is to tell the reader of her own experience. She probably felt she had at least *touched* all these stages she so vividly describes.

If you are not a Roman Catholic you get the definite impression these are *the* stages which *all* believers *must* pass through. This simply is not true. The New Testament establishes no such formulas. *There is no formula in transformation.* The Lord, like C. S. Lewis' Aslan, is not tame—He is not a God of formulas. He is a living God and a vital, living experience; He is experienced in different ways daily. Not a "something" out there which is revealed by going through a series of preset steps. *Spiritual Torrents* is the personal experience of a woman on her way to God.

In my judgement, her detailing of Christian suffering is both Guyon's greatest strength and her greatest weakness. A friend of mine, commenting on a chapter entitled "Dark Night of the Spirit" in my book, *the Inward Journey*, probably summed up this paradox. He said, "Gene, people who have never gone through what you described there have no idea of what you are talking about; and those of us who have, surely don't want to read about it."

There it is.

Reading Guyon's vivid, sometimes morose descriptions of her experiences—if you are unfamiliar with her life and writings—will leave you not knowing how to react.

There are *three* kinds of people who I wish would never find a book like this. (I am speaking here particularly of deeply damaged people. I remind you that this book did not damage them. Books don't make people odd; odd people just get more articulate in demonstrating how odd they are after reading a book like this.)

First, there is the religious single brother. He should not read this book. All super-religious single brothers should get married! After ten years of marriage this book could not possibly hurt them! Unmarried, young brother, if you are inclined to be "religious," then this book is going to make you downright intolerable. Please remember, when you are all tied up in little knots because you have in some terrible way failed to live up to some self-established standard, you are obviously not making spiritual progress. And when you discern that you are making progress, get puffed up and legalistic, and start adjusting everyone else, you are *still* not making spiritual progress! There is one very redeeming thing about this book: Spiritual stages, which some Christians plan to zip through in a weekend—Guyon assures you they will take twenty to thirty years!

The second kind of person who should not read this kind of book is the truly psychotic. Religious people who are also psychotic seem often to be people in their thirties and forties. What more can I say? This type person causes anyone who has ever written a Christian book, no matter how bland the book nor how mild the subject, to severely question if he should ever write another book again. There are disturbed people who are damaged by *any* Christian literature they read.

Last of all there is the pompous, blind, self-deluded Christian who lives in vain visions of self-grandeur, who sees himself (or herself) as a second Jeanne Guyon: "I have read this book; I have gone through all these stages, and today I am . . . " Well, not every one of these folks is quite that open about it, but they ooze the message from every pore in their bodies: "I have arrived."

Perhaps I should try not only to de-fang this book but also do a little de-fanging of a few Christians.

I will state, first of all, that all spiritual pursuit should be done inside an experience of church life, never privately on your own alone. The church is where spiritual pursuits belong.

Secondly I would like to share with you that I live among people who seek a deeper walk with the Lord. (I number myself among those seekers.) From one end of this broad world to another, whenever I have traveled, if time permitted, I have sought out godly men and women. But I have known only two people in my life whom I would call spiritually mature. Two, I repeat, Two! Both would be horrified at the thought that anyone would so classify them. One was a woman, Beta Shyrick by name. She was a profound influence on my life. (She never arrived at a point, by the way, which Jeanne Guyon describes as "indifference.") Beta died at 76 of a broken heart.

My point? I don't hold your spiritual interpretation of yourself very high. You most likely aren't really all that spiritual. Certainly, I would not recommend you try to figure out what "stage" you are in. Quite frankly, for myself, I am sure of only one: I have been redeemed by Christ. Beyond that point all is a little hazy to me. Over against those two Christians I met who showed some element of Christian maturity, I have met a backyard full of Christians who thought they were spiritual! I have to admit that in a real way this book is ideal for them. It is either going to so expose their gross spiritual inadequacies as to leave them speechless or it will add to their self-delusion.

It is in that respect that *Spiritual Torrents* is a very excellent book. It should leave us all a little more humble about what the process of transformation can *really* entail.

That brings me to another reason for republishing *Spiritual Torrents*. I have been ministering on the deeper aspects of the Christian faith for . . . well, a long time. Long enough to have discovered patterns of reactions in those who have set out, in their youth, on this great adventure.

I have watched Christians be drawn so close to Christ in a living relationship, closer than they ever dreamed possible. I have watched them revel in discovery of the profound, indescribable riches which are in Christ. During all that time those Christians, with these riches, were daily being reminded of the cross, suffering, and the duplicity of the human heart—most of all, the cross. Each was reminded that those rich days of intimacy would *not*—could not—last forever. Dry spells would also have to be known. Yet I have seen a few Christians, when those wonderful waters receded, stop following the Lord. Most Christians *do* continue through the dry spells, but so many, when they finally met the cross in its full devastating power, stopped following Him. Almost all, it seems, will vow and declare they never heard anyone warn them about such trials or a cross so great!

Well, dear readers, meet Jeanne Guyon in *Spiritual*

Torrents. Here is a master (nay! a past-master) at describing the cross. This book will drown you in the details of suffering.

The first half of this book may leave you depressed; it may leave you with a distorted idea of God . . . and of the whole Christian life. But it will never leave you unwarned.

1

As soon as God touches a seeker, He gives that new believer an instinct to return to Him more perfectly and be united with Him. There is something within the believer that knows he has not been created for amusement or the trivials of the world but has an end which is centered in His Lord. Something within the believer endeavors to cause him to return to a place deep within, to a place of rest. It is an instinctive thing, this pull to return to God. Some receive it in a larger portion, according to God's design, others to a smaller degree, by God's design. But each believer has that loving impatience to return to his source of origin.

Therefore a Christian might be compared to a river. The river comes forth from its source and flows relentlessly to the sea. One river flows majestically, slowly. Another flows very rapidly. There are also some rivers which flow as a torrent, running with impetuosity as though there were nothing that could check them. Dikes may be erected, other hindrances to the course may be found, but this only doubles the river's determination to plunge into the sea.

We who are believers are like rivers. There are rivers that flow very slowly, arriving late to their destination. Others move more rapidly than that. The third type moves so fast that none dare sail upon it. It is a mad, headlong torrent.

It is the purpose of this small writing that we might look at these three figures and learn from each of them.

2

Here is the Christian who, after he is converted, gives some time to be in his Lord's presence. His words are measured and he seeks to purify himself, to remove himself from outward and outstanding sins. He has set his course to move forward little by little.

This believer can be greatly curtailed by a drought. In fact, there are times when the riverbed is completely dry. Sometimes it seems this river is no longer flowing from the source form which it came. There is no transportation that can be placed upon this river because the river is slow and because sometimes it is quite empty.

But there is great help for such a river. Such a river can always join course with another small tributary and together, by helping one another, they move forward to their destination.

Why the slowness? Is it because this believer is not engaged in an internal walk? His labor is on the outside and seldom goes beyond the most objective prayer. Surely such a believer is as sanctified as are others. God gives them light to adapt to the state which they have chosen. Such a believer can sometimes be quite beautiful and often gains the admiration of others.

Sometimes such a one will receive some light that suddenly hurries him on; nonetheless, most never get out of themselves. This Christian often has a thousand holy intentions of seeking his Lord. Most, however, do their seeking after God according to their own efforts.

If someone seeks to help this Christian to a deeper relationship with the Lord he will probably not succeed. There are several reasons for this. First, the Christian who would call this believer forth has nothing supernatural to offer; and, be assured, it is often an absorption with supernatural things which drives this weak believer on.

Secondly, if you will observe, this believer has a great capacity to reason. He is usually strong in this area. He can be, and often is, very strong willed . . . even in his determination to pursue the Lord. But it is an objective pursuit. The more mature Christian may find

4

that, in seeking to help this believer, he is dealing with one who swings from one extreme to another in his spiritual experience. He has many high places and many low places. Sometimes he is an absolute wonder in his progress and at other times he is very weak. When in a low place this one will fall into great discouragement. *He possesses no deep peace or calm in the presence of distraction.* You will also find that he is willing to combat anything that comes his way and he *also* complains about things that come his way.

It is safer if this believer does not learn quickly about an internal walk. Why? Because you have taken from him the means he has chosen to move toward his Lord. If you remove those things he leans on, you may leave that believer with nothing to hold to in his forward course with God. Perhaps in this very fact we find some of the reasons for disputes among Christians concerning the proper way to walk with the Lord. Those who have found a deeper element in their relationship with their God recognize the good that they have derived from it and, therefore, they wish everyone else to walk this way. On the other hand the more objective believer has found his way of walking with the Lord quite sufficient and would seek to make everyone comply with *his* way. What is the solution? The solution is to discern which type of Christian you are dealing with. Whichever it is, help him along in a way which *he has chosen*. After all, this is the way which best suits his inborn disposition.

You need only watch. There are many believers who simply cannot come into the Lord's presence, quiet themselves before Him, and stay for a long period of time.

There are others who have a great gift of covering up their faults, not only from others but from themselves as well. You will find those believers, generally, to be completely wrapped up in human emotions and feelings. Both the rational person and the emotional person are attached very much to their reasoning.

Must they continue ever so? Can they be helped further along? Yes, but it takes a wise person to render such help. To show the believer how to walk according to the whole extent of the divine will, you must neither run before grace nor refuse to follow it. Ours is to *correspond* with the grace of God.

Unfortunately, many Christians, in seeking to help another Christian to know the Lord better, find that they have reached the end of their abilities; and rather than helping him further or, perhaps mercifully, leaving him alone, they decide to bring him into their own orb and make him their follower—not the Lord's follower.

Each of us as believers needs to be shown how to reason less and love more. Sometimes this has to be done very, very slowly for our proneness to reasoning goes very deep. If a believer will respond to learning how to *love* his Lord, then surely he can advance toward his Lord. *There* is his help.

On the other hand, the believer may begin literally to dry up when he forsakes his reasoning. If this happens, he cannot lay hold of a more passionate, deep love for his Lord. In such a case it is wise to encourage this believer to a more active and objective walk with his Lord. If he cannot reach his Lord in a deep spiritual understanding, he can at least serve Him by his will.

You see, there are two ways that we respond to dryness. One is to lose all heart and hope. The other is to instinctively know that the dryness is from the Lord and, therefore, continue to follow after Him, *even in the dry places.* The believer who cannot respond to a dry spell in this way should be encouraged to run the race with all his strength until it pleases God to relieve him of his labors—that is, until this little streamlet finds the river and is received into its bosom and carried to the sea.

I have often wondered why there is an outcry against spiritual books and such opposition to Christians who write and speak on an

7

internal walk in the Lord. It is my judgement that such a writer or speaker can do no harm. The only person who will be harmed is someone who is self-seeking in the first place. But the humble soul who desires to know his Lord better and realizes he is not going to receive this gift on his own and must have help from some other source . . . should he be forbidden to hear or to read?

What of the Christian who will read a book and deceive himself into talking and acting as though he has attained some spiritual level, using a "spiritual" vocabulary, seeming to have entered some spiritual place?

Well, even a Christian of average discernment can tell when such a state is not reality.

I have a second reason for believing that books on the internal walk are not harmful. Books encourage the reader to separate from the world, to understand the meaning of death. By such reading, a believer gains insight into things that need to be conquered, things that need to be destroyed. In reading these books the Christian begins to realize he does not have enough strength for such undertakings, and therefore he will begin to turn to the indwelling Christ and to draw from Him the strength for such a venture.

No Christian should ever undertake to be his own spiritual leader, especially when he has a very religious nature. He needs to realize that he needs the help of someone else to lead him on his way to the Spirit of God. There are, of course, dangers in turning to someone else for spiritual leadership. A believer may turn to someone who is seeking to appropriate followers to himself. Such a person will, of course, put limits to the grace of God and fix barriers that prevent the believer from advancing. Often this Christian leader believes that *there is only one way . . . his way!* He would fain make the whole world walk in that way alone. There is great mischief in this. The leader who fixes all things on the deeper life and yet establishes one certain direction prevents God from communicating to the seeker.

Perhaps we should do for the spiritual life what we do in schools. The student is not always kept in the same class, but is transferred each year to a higher class. The teacher in the sixth grade does not teach what has been presented in the fifth. Human education is of so little value, and yet so much care is given to it. Divine science is so important and so necessary, yet so neglected. Shall there never be a school for prayer? But, alas! Those who seek to study prayer only spoil it. They teach prayer and then set up rules and measure the Spirit of God. But the Spirit is without measure, nor is He confined to rules.

I would urge you to see that there is no such

thing as a believer who is incapable of knowing the Lord, to some measure, in a deeper way. There is no reason for any of us, no matter what our disposition or background, not to apply ourselves to know the Lord more personally or intimately. The dullest person is capable of such. I know this because I have seen it. There have been those people who have sought me out who seemed almost incapable of spiritual insight and who also seemed unwilling to pursue any spiritual adventure, and those who, having attempted a spiritual venture, after some time decided to give up the whole matter entirely. Despite this, and their repugnance, they continued and made a little advance. I have seen these people, after the passing of several years, reach a high degree of spiritual attainment. Often these with whom I have dealt have said to me that they would have given up if they had not had my help. Now what would have happened if someone, having watched them for four or five years making no progress, would have told them that they simply could not be warmed with the Love of God? Or perhaps they would have said to them, "You have simply not been called to this kind of relationship with Christ."

I address you, the believer: You, as much as anyone else, are fit to know God's design for your life. If you are faithful you may come to know Him better than those with great intellect and reasoning . . . those who would rather study about prayer and spiritual matters than to experience them. It does not matter how poor you feel you may be. You are well adapted to know the Lord if you will do but one thing: Do not grow weary; wait humbly in His presence until the door opens.

On the other hand, those of great reasoning and understanding seem to be unable to maintain even a moment of silence before God. Such a Christian has an admirable facility to bring forth a stream of words, knows how to pray, knows all the parts of prayer, can speak clearly and exactly on all spiritual subjects and seems to be very well pleased with himself that he can do these things. And yet ten or twenty years later that person will be in the same place in his spiritual life that he is today.

Which of the two is more qualified to pursue the inward way?

Is it not true, even on the human level, that the most wretched creature who sets out to love does so without a plan or a method? The most ignorant in the matter of love is often the most skilled. The same is true, except on a vastly higher level, in dealing with the matter of divine love.

I would address you who lead other Christians in their walk with Christ! A person comes to you who knows little of the deeper things of Christ. You need to do only one thing: teach him to love God. Teach him how to cast himself headlong into that love. He will soon be a conqueror. And if he seems to be someone who is well adapted to love, allow him to do his best, and wait in patience until love itself will make him *love!* And let him love his Lord in his own way and not in your way.

Oh, my God, when will men understand to teach others how to testify to love.

3

We look now at the second river. Here is a large river that moves with a steady pace, that flows with pomp and majesty. The course of this river is easily distinguished. There is order there. The river is laden with ships and merchants carrying their goods upon it. Some of these rivers make it to the sea, losing themselves, for the most part, in a greater river or ending up in some tributary of the sea. Tragically, many such a river serves only to carry merchandise and commerce.

This river can be checked; it can be slowed down by a dam or a dike; it can be turned aside at certain places.

The source of this river is very abundant; there is much gift there, much grace and many heavenly favors. There are many saints in the church of God who shine as brilliant stars and yet they never pass the degree of this river.

In fact there are two such kinds of rivers, two kinds of Christians who fall into this category. There are those whom the Lord pities because of labor for Him, despite the fact they are dry and arid. Little by little He draws such a one by His goodness and by the richness of His life.

The second group of Christians is seized by the heart almost at the outset. They feel a sense of loving Him but never become intimately acquainted with the object of their love. Human love supposes a knowledge of the object of its love. That is, in human love we know the one we love. Without that intimate knowledge, human love simply cannot be, because what the eye sees, the heart can know. This is not the way of divine love. The Lord has control over our hearts; therefore, the Lord is not obligated to allow us to know Him well. In fact, there are times when He can cause the heart to love Him when the heart knows hardly anything about Him!

If you are helping other Christians to find their way to the Lord, you will one day meet a believer who seems to be passionately in love with his Lord and yet who knows little of Him. This type of Christian makes a great deal of progress toward the Lord. He seems to have a wonderful relationship with Him and to be in complete consort with His will. And yet there seems to be something within that is never truly dealt with, never annihilated.

It seems that God does not usually take this one out of his selfhood that he might totally lose himself in God. There is simply a fervent love, and as a result, such a believer excites the admiration and astonishment of others. God gives him graces upon graces and gifts upon gifts, light upon light. There are visions and revelations. This one often hears the voice of the Lord. There is so much, it even seems the Lord has no other care except to enrich and beautify this person and to communicate with this person His secrets. All light seems to be in this believer.

This believer has temptation, yet the temptation is repelled with vigor. The cross is borne with strength. Such a Christian even wishes there would be more of the cross! This one is all fire and all flame and all love. Here is a believer with a great heart, ready to undertake anything. He is, in fact, a prodigy in the age in which he lives. The Lord uses such people to do miracles. It seems that all they need do is to desire something and God grants it—that He delights in nothing else than granting them their desires and fulfilling their wills.

Furthermore, they are in a high degree of self-sacrifice. They are not of this world and practice austerity.

If such a Christian, in his youth, comes to you seeking the Lord, you may help him greatly or you may hurt him greatly. One thing you can do to hurt him is to show how much you admire him. In so doing you divert his mind to himself. Such a Christian will then come to rest in the *gifts* of God instead of being made to run after the Lord Himself.

You see, the great grace which the Lord has given these saints is given in order to draw them to Him. This Christian runs a great risk in resting in his gifts, pondering his gifts, looking at them and then, tragically, appropriating them to himself. Out of this comes vanity and self-complacency, preferences for one's own self over another, and often, the ruin of one's interior spiritual life.

When a Christian of this temperament has reached a higher plane with the Lord, he can sometimes be quite helpful to the newer Christian (but not so much as the Christian whom we will be looking at in the next chapter). The reason is *this Christian is very strong* in God. And he sometimes *cannot understand* the weaknesses of others. For instance, a Mother Superior may be a Christian of this kind and, therefore, find it hard to have motherly compassion for the weak. Such a Christian can be quite astonished at the confessions they hear from weaker believers.

A person of this disposition often expects a high degree of perfection from others and cannot lead a believer in the course of "little by little." Such a person simply is lacking when working with those who are terribly imperfect. Such a one often works best alone and accomplishes much in his charity toward God in this manner.

Should such a Christian speak to you, you may come to believe he is very advanced in spiritual attainment, perhaps even to total attainment. The vocabulary is there—the cross, death, loss, love; and what he speaks is true and, in his own way, he has experienced each one of these. And he has lost himself in God. His desires are very lofty. Perhaps there is a lacking here that only the divine eye of God can discover. A large number of Christians who have been admired throughout the ages are those who have walked in the Lord in this way. Nonetheless, this believer has been laden with so much merchandise that his course upon the river is extremely slow. What can be done with such a Christian? Will such Christians forever go this way?

They will unless there is some miracle of providence, unless they are led by someone who is profoundly enlightened in the Lord's inner way, someone to show them that they are neither to resist nor to look at their gifts, but to go *beyond* them.

The Christian laden with merchandise is himself somewhat of a dam which keeps the water from flowing on its way, simply because there is so much, wittingly or unwittingly, of looking at himself.

If you are helping a new Christian into a deeper walk with his God, do not appeal to his reasoning ability, do not sharpen his reasoning ability; but seek to lead him from there to more spiritually perceived matters. Turn him to faith, to the very deep and uncertain darkness of depending wholly on his faith in his Lord. Do not ask him to write down what his knowledge is, for he should not build anything on knowledge but on providence.

Surely, it is good to know the ways of God, but the Lord alone ought to furnish the ways. There seem to be so many ways to the Lord, especially for those who seem not to have received a great deal of instruction in the *internal* way. They are abundant with ways to God and methods for all purposes.

There are those who do not turn to the Lord in serious concentration until after some deep internal experience in which death touches their inward parts. Often such a person has almost an intuitive understanding of the Lord, but it is an insight into the Lord that needs much tutoring. They perceive much but the depth is more limited than they realize. I would say to the person who is helping such a believer; if he is gifted, do not regret it when you have seen his gifts and graces falling apart, because such things are hidden in God's own providence.

4

The third Christian is one who moves down the mountains like a torrent. This Christian has his source from the Lord. Nothing stops him. He runs with a boldness that strikes fear in the boldest Christian. The person I am describing in this third stage seems to have extraordinary relationships with providence. The events that fall into his life are extreme and violent. He is irregular in his path. Sometimes he passes through ground not firm and picks up impurities. Sometimes he is lost in the deep underground riverbeds and is not found for considerable distances. Then he may emerge only briefly to be swallowed up in yet another cavern. But at last he comes to the sea, and there he is in his happiest state for he is swallowed up in the sea, never again to find himself. He becomes part of the sea itself; and, whereas the other river might carry great merchandise upon its back, here, as part of the sea, this torrent now helps in holding up the largest ships that sail on the ocean. Its capacity is without limits for it is part of the sea itself.

Previously, the merchants could make no use of the river while it was a torrent. And now it is lost to the visible eye within the sea.

I would like to now trace the experience and course of this river (this Christian) from the moment of his conversion to the time when the river is lost in the sea. What process does such a Christian follow, and by what degree-upon-degree does he move toward his Lord? What are the aspects of his adventure to the sea?

If you are this Christian, your source is God. He is also your end. In the beginning you are checked by sin. Your heart is in perpetual motion and cannot find its rest, for its rest is in God alone. If you are seeking rest in this life you will never find it except inside of your Lord. Your seeking then must be the ends of God. You will notice that fire is very active on the outer edges, but its source is light.

As soon as sin ceases to hold you back you can run to find your Lord. If you could be exempt from sin, which you cannot be, how swift would be your destination! The nearer you would approach the center of God the more your speed would increase and the race be peaceful.

You have a fire and are continually putting wood upon it to prevent it from mounting upward. There are obstacles that must be removed. You, by nature, are inclined toward your Lord. Were it not for hindrances you would run unceasingly toward Him. If you are sinning unnecessarily, you are arresting your progress toward your goal. You will advance by little or by much according to the obstacles you put in your way yourself.

But those believers who consider themselves good because they have not known many weaknesses have many problems, too. Take, for instance, the virgin, or someone who has taken chastity as a vow. Be careful that you do not make purity your idol. Remember, your Lord makes His mercies abound where sin has abounded. Be careful that you do not love your own righteousness. It is an obstacle that is more difficult to get around than the greatest of sins.

You will never know the center of God by an exalted view of yourself.

The barrier is simply too great. You must have neither strong attachment to sin nor to your own righteousness. The Lord will never allow you to take true pleasure in such a view of yourself.

One of the first things the Lord does to you is to make you sense that you are estranged from the Lord. This causes you to search out your inmost being for sin in your life and to grieve often over these sins with a great deal of anguish and pain. You may glimpse that far off place of rest, but it only increases your restlessness; however, it also increases your desire to pursue after that repose.

You may find that you will, at this point, begin looking for some way to touch the Lord internally. This may cause you to turn to a very objective type of prayer, to meditation, or many other adaptations and Christian exercise. You will probably find these all to be wanting, and this venture will only serve to increase even more your desire to know Him better. And if you happen to be successful in whatever it is you try, you must realize you have only soothed the disease, not healed it. If you try to fight the situation, you will only redouble your impatience.

If a Christian in this state does not find someone who can help him along further, he will lose a great deal of time. But be sure that the Lord in His providence will *let this time be transitory.* It will pass. One way or the other He meets this Christian's need. And usually He does so, not in any extraordinary way, but in some way that is quite natural.

Sometimes the person trying to lead this Christian to know his Lord better is himself quite wanting in his ability to do that very thing. Often this seeking Christian will discover on his own, in astonishment, surprise and delight, that he has within his own self the very treasure he was seeking. The Christian now discovers that prayer does not have to be a costly and boring thing, and he rejoices in his newfound liberty. He goes deep within and there finds the Lord. He find indescribable delight that carries him away. He wishes to stay in this state (the state of love and inward dwelling) forever.

I would observe here that as delightful as this state would appear, the Christian is nonetheless dealing with something with which he is not well acquainted. He is filled with ardor and love. He feels that he is in paradise. He has found within him something sweeter than all the pleasures of earth, and he would leave the world to enjoy his inmost experiences. His prayer almost becomes uninterrupted. His love increases from day to day. Everything that burdened him drops away. Left to his own designs, he would accept the love of the Lord perpetually and allow no interruptions.

That in itself is a sign of his weakness. He is afraid of conversation. He is afraid of any type of commerce with other people. He has a fragile relationship with the Lord that he fears can be dispelled very easily. If he does fall into sin he will always consider it very serious sin. He heaps upon himself the greatest chastisement and will reprove himself for an idle word or an idle thought. What shall we say but this: that it is up to the Lord alone to continue his work in this soul and to purify him.

If the Lord seems to leave this poor believer, then that believer is swallowed up in confusion. Once restored to fellowship he wants to exhort everyone to love God.

Some would close their eyes and be blind and dumb in this state, that they might not hinder the joy they are knowing. They are like people possessed with wine. Reading a single line is illumination enough; it would take a whole day to read a page. One word of the Lord awakens the instinct toward Him which inflames the heart.

At this point objective and vocal prayer simply is not something the believer will find palatable. Some are confused as to why they can no longer pray. This one simply knows he cannot pray with his mouth. Something sweet and loving has kept him in silence. Seeking to be objective in prayer now would cause the loss of his heavenly peace and introduce a sense of spiritual dryness.

If you are working with someone who is going through this stage (this torrential plunge into God) do not hinder him by encouraging vocal and objective praying. The Christian becomes extremely sensitive to sin; and when suffering comes into his life he has no prayer within him which asks for a shortening of that suffering.

If you were to ask this believer about his present experience, he would surely tell you that he has reached the very center of God and that he is so tranquil and delighted with his Lord he is sure he has reached some ultimate pinnacle. He sees nothing more to do but to enjoy the state he is in.

Many, many Christians truly believe this *is* the ultimate goal God has for us, and proclaim the gospel this way.

And how long does such a stage (or degree) last in a Christian's life? Perhaps for a long time. There are Christians who never reach beyond this experience in their lives . . . they are sometimes admired by all mankind, and some are even sainted!

It is true that the Christian in this stage will know short periods of dryness but such an event does not cause him to fall backward but only to move forward and upward.

Nonetheless, the Christian is content and is enjoying his Lord and is enjoying those things he believes to be the Lord. But note this. If you were to take that state away from the believer he would feel he had fallen into irreparable misfortune.

Let's look further at the imperfection of this stage.

5

While this river—this Christian—was still on the mountain, he was peaceful, enjoying rest, and never had any thought of falling. Nonetheless, by the very intensity of his experience, this river—this Christian—has a spiritual instinct to turn more and more to the Lord within his center. *This* is a gift of faith. But as he seeks to express his faith he may unknowingly cause something of his rest and trust in the Lord to start seeping away. The water is still moving, but it is not moving toward the sea. There is something amiss. It is moving toward its inevitable destruction.

He may wish to return to the mountain where he had been, but this is now no longer possible.

There will be level spots ahead; there the river will find rest. But, be sure, there is a tumult ahead. Again and again the Christian will mistake these areas of rest as being a time when he has been able to reclaim that which he once had. He will be certain that the treacherous falls he has recently been through have purified him. But the imperfections are still there. Further, there is *much more* that must be done in this believer's life. I must warn you that the Christian can truly believe his suffering is over in these respites.

Poor torrent, you think that you have found rest. You are beginning to take pleasure in your own waters. You gaze at yourself in a mirror which these waters make and think yourself most fair. What is your surprise, when in flowing along so smoothly over the sand, you meet unexpectedly a downward fall yet steeper and longer and more dangerous than those which you have already experienced.

The river cannot even find its riverbeds now; it falls from rock to rock. There is no order nor reason. Others hear the noise and are even afraid to approach.

Oh, torrent what will you do? You see the great fall you are going through and believe yourself lost. Do not fear, you are not lost. This and other falls that remain further out are for your better redemption.

Eventually the Christian—the river—feels that he has reached the lower part of the mountain and is in level country. Again there is calmness. Now the Christian has entered yet another stage in his spiritual experience. He will perhaps find rest again and it may even last for many years. Gradually, however, the believer becomes aware that he is experiencing, again, inclinations for things that he thought had long since left. He is shocked! Peace again seems to slip away as distractions seem to come in hordes. There are seasons of drought and dryness. Instead of bread there are only stones. Prayer becomes a disagreeable thing at best. Passion, which he thought was dead, comes back to life.

The Christian is astounded. He would either return to that place from which he has fallen or at least stay where he is and fall no further. But the end of the mountain has been reached. Mountaintop experiences will be no more! The soul must now take a great plunge. The Christian holds back, clinging to some precious past devotion. He redoubles his repentance, grasps at anything anyone has ever taught him about how to maintain the faith and how to return to the Lord. Everything he tries to do is labor. In all this he feels that somewhere he is at fault. "Something is amiss in my life that is causing all of this. If only I can put it right."

The believer now faces what seems to him to be an obvious fact—that he is going to receive no help from the Lord. The unfaithfulness of God frightens him. He laments the loss of the (felt) presence of his Lord. *But to the astonishment of the Christian the Lord does return.*

At this point the Christian makes the mistake of believing the dark days are over, that the Lord has brought new blessings, and that a new purity has been, and will be, established. He believes he has truly come to distrust his own self life.

This new relationship the Christian has with his Lord is now greatly prized and considered to be a fragile thing. He does not run tempestuously as he had before. He does not want to lose the treasure which he once thought he had lost. He is more sensitive about displeasing his Lord, lest the Lord would withdraw from him. He endeavors to be more faithful than ever before.

Despite this more cautious walk, being in such fellowship with the Lord once more begins to cause the Christian to believe he can take this present state for granted. The delights he knows are even better, in his judgement, than those before because they have come with much suffering. He sees himself in a new walk with the Lord; a new rest has come.

Alas, the Christian is about to see an even greater descent. One ever longer and steeper than the last.

Peace is gone. What formerly gave life now brings death. An agitation now runs deeper than ever before; he discovers he can hardly establish any relationship with the cross at all. The Christian doubles his commitment to patience. He weeps and groans. He is cast down. He complains to his Lord that he has been abandoned. His complaints are not heard. The more the trouble, the more the complaints. All efforts at "being good" are now difficult. A tendency to other things has set in.

The fear of returning to worldliness causes the Christian to redouble his efforts to remain a Christian in his walk. The dove has gone forth from the ark but cannot find a place upon the earth to rest. It seems when the dove returns, Noah has closed the doors and windows. It can only hover, seeking rest but unable to find it. Eventually the Lord, in his mercy, opens that door and accepts the believer once again fully.

Can you not see that all this is divine and loving goodness? This is simply the way the Lord deals with the soul. He does these things that the river might move more rapidly toward

Him. He flees, He hides, that He might draw the believer after Him. He lets him fall (apparently that He and He alone might have the privilege of lifting him up. He is seeking to show that He, *alone*, is the incontestable strength of the Christian.

If you are one of those who is strong and vigorous and never has known these experiences (these devices of love, these events which seem so loving as others watch but seem so terrible to the one experiencing them), to you I would say, "You have never experienced the utter limits of your own weakness, nor do you know the great need that you have of His aid."

The poor soul that goes through these experiences begins to lean no longer upon himself but upon his Beloved. The severity with which the Lord sometimes deals with His child only makes the Lord Himself more desirable.

Still, the Christian, when he finds his Lord has withdrawn, believes it is his fault. He tries to mend his way with everyone and everything. But the more the Christian runs the more he remains where he is.

Oh, Dear Lord, that these souls could be reduced to power, a state that is better than a thousand states of repentance intended to repair the injury they feel they have done to Thee.

If the Lord should come and bring an end to this agitated state, it is only that the believer might have a little rest. Unknowingly, the Christian *is* advancing, and those little moments of rest and respite come more briefly and are more fragile.

Finally, one thing comes into view. The Christian realizes that there is something within him that needs to die. Prayer, devotion, conversation, *everything* has the taste of death upon it. If the Christian really has a heart for the Lord, then he may find himself in a place were *everything* seems to have lost meaning.

After having fought so long and so hard there comes now a succession of sorrow and rest, of dying and then living. The Christian begins to see a little of what is going on in his life. He realizes those periods of death are working for him; for, in those small times when the Lord is with him, there is a greater purity in the relationship. And the rest is a deeper rest. Perhaps more short-lived, true, but also more pure and profound. The Christian begins to understand that something of the Lord is working death into his being . . . and that this is wholly in the hands of God, and that it is a thing that is *good*.

The Christian is beginning to learn to let the Lord come and go as *He* wills, and to learn that it is not necessary to be possessed with the Lord's presence.

And now let us discuss the reason for all these discoveries! The believer is now being slowly prepared for a little more progress in his life. The Christian may not realize it, but he is actually moving toward that great sea. His rests are shorter and simpler. Enjoyment is less but it is pure. The route seems to be filled with anguish, but there is a certain kind of joy in knowing that the Lord has laid aside certain distractions, and perhaps those former stages will never return again.

6

You will be surprised at what is said next.

At the very moment in his travels as a torrent when the believer seems to be dying and is about to breathe his last, he suddenly recovers and lays hold of new strength. It is like a lamp that has exhausted its oil. Just before the light goes out a flame spurts up. But sooner or later the flame will die. There will be a recovery, but it may not last for a long time.

The river is frozen over now. It is all ice. It seems there is no movement. Even slight warmth would cause this river to think itself on fire.

We are looking here at a love which is gentle but appears very cold.

Have You loved us only to leave us? You wound the soul and then cause it to run after the Author of the wound. You draw us after You. You show us Yourself. And when we have possessed You, You flee away. And, then when You have seen us reduced to our extremities, having lost all breath with which to run, You show Yourself, for a moment, that we may recover life. You depart again, and dying becomes an even more rigorous thing. O harsh Love, O innocent Destroyer, why do You not slay at once? You give wine to the dying soul! The wine imparts life anew, then You wrest it away again. Is this your sport? You seem to heal the wound and then inflict a new one. In ordinary death, men die but once and the pain is over. When the criminal dies, all are satisfied that they have destroyed him but once. Thou, O Lord, with less pity, take life from us a thousand times, and then give it back anew.

O life, life which we cannot lose unless there are many deaths—O death, special and precious death, we cannot have unless we lose so many lives.

Lord, you will come to the end of this life; but what is the good of it? When the body dies it loses all sensation. Not so with the soul. It goes on suffering even after death. There is a nothingness that is vastly more painful than death could ever be.

Here is a situation that has astonished many a Christian: to look at a friend who has lived a holy life, even like the angels, and then see him go through unending distress. Men have no way to account for all this, for it is not according to their theology nor their understanding of God.

This period in the seeker's life can last for a long time. Consequently, when I meet with someone who speaks of making a very rapid advancement, I cannot help saying that that person may be naive. True, such persons may seem perfect. Their internal relationship with the Lord is flawless. But for them to think that they have passed this period to which I am presently referring is a mistake. They may wake up one day and be astonished to discover ways of God which they never dreamed existed.

I would pause here to say, when you are a young Christian starting out in your adventure with Christ and you are making a great deal of progress, you may feel *that you are far advanced beyond* where you *really* are! Be careful not to apply to yourself a stage of Christian growth that you are not really in, nor to read into your experience more than is truly there. This is a pitfall of all too many Christians.

For instance, do not seek to strip your soul of all things except the Lord. That must be left to God alone to do. To try to do so yourself is dangerous. But this is a lesson quite difficult to learn. The Lord will take away from you exactly what He wishes to take. And He will do it in a perfect way. To seek to do this on your own is to spoil the divine work.

There are so many Christians who begin to learn a little about an inward walk with the Lord, they hear something about "the soul being stripped of all," and they set out to do it themselves. Even then they say they are leaving it to the Lord to do. There is no progress in this. He neither allows us to unclothe ourselves nor to clothe ourselves. It is *He* who impoverishes, and *He* does so to make us rich. The person who seeks this on his own gains nothing.

Even to seek to empty, to impoverish and to kill is, in that very act, preserving life. Yes, you are actually preserving a portion of your life which ought to be laid down. *You* are doing it. This is a ghastly mistake that speaks of much self-life and much blindness!

You will notice that if you wish to put out a lamp, you may do two things: extinguish it or simply refrain from putting oil in it. In this way it goes out on its own. But if, in your choice to allow the lamp to go out, you keep putting oil in it from time to time, the lamp will never go out.

Leave the Lord to do these things. If, when the Lord's stripping comes to you, you seek to put just a little oil in to make the suffering more comfortable, you are wasting time, and you are wasting the Lord's work in your life. You are only postponing a death. You are putting off an inevitable funeral. If you will not fight the death which the Lord has chosen for certain parts of your nature, then that death will result in life.

Some, when drowning, struggle to reach the shallows. Such a person will hold to anything he can find. He drowns when he is exhausted. Are you one of those who fight to his uttermost that you may not perish? You will die only from *lack* of strength! Sometimes the Lord numbs the hands and arms, or even cuts them off, compelling you thus to sink to the bottom. You cry out with all strength, but in vain. You are faced with a God who is without pity, yet it is His great mercy which has nothing to give to the self-nature in its last throes of sinking.

And again I would address those who are seeking to guide other Christians. I would not recommend succor to those who come to this state. You cannot contribute to death's work within their hearts. Neither can you effectively rescue them from the Lord's mighty hands.

If this person is one who is *truly* seeking after the Lord and *truly* comitted to Him, *love* will not even give the dying one burial.

If the Christian goes on in his course, he will meet the cross again and again. It seems that the cross even multiplies. If you follow this Christian long enough in his downward plunge, you will notice he seems to become almost without feeling toward the finer sense of things spiritual. In fact, the Christian settles down to become accustomed to his pain, his impotence and his uselessness. He *is* despair itself. He consents to the loss of God's favor. He may even think that God has taken away divine favor *justly* because of his own wickedness. There is no thought or hope of ever seeing joy again. To meet some victorious or gracious Christian now is simply double pain. The believer drops into the deeper depths of nothingness.

*That which I have feared the most
has come upon me.—Job*

"What is it," he cries, "to lose God forever, without hope of ever finding Him again? to be deprived of all love for all time and eternity? To be no longer able to love Him who is so lovely?"

Ah, this is the soul's lament, the psalm of the (seemingly) forsaken Christian.

The Christian truly believes that this is what has happened to him. *He does not realize that he has never loved so strongly as now; nor has he ever loved so purely.* He may have lost the vigor to love, and the sense of love, and the power to love; but he has not lost the love itself.

He has *never* loved more truly.

Of course, the poor soul cannot believe all this. Yet it is a plain fact. Do you see, this believer cannot exist without love. If he did not love God, he would go and love something else. But here is one who is not taking pleasure in *anything* whatsoever! Mark this, he has *not* left the race . . . as so many others have. He believes he is dying without God; but God is his lament . . . his one and only thought. Nevertheless, he cannot see this.

True, there are still problems with sin and the world, but this causes him great grief. He revolts at his lusts and his involuntary faults and sees them as dreadful things. He no sooner washes himself than he falls back into what he feels is some sewer.

The Christian simply does not know what to do any longer. Earlier he was self-confident. He had appropriated the gifts of God. (But he had simply fallen into self-love.) Should he have sought to truly run farther and deeper, so greatly endowed, he would have been impeded by such a load. In fact, if he had not lost *all* (all his riches which he had in his relationship with his Lord), his very fear of losing those riches would have hindered him from running the course. But no longer, for all now *is* lost!

This Christian is as a once beautiful bride whose groom was delighted. Now she is naked and tattered and torn. What has become of her?

Here is the explanation. The Lord saw this one's beauty, but He also saw that she amused herself with her ornaments, taking pleasure in them. She thought she was looking upon Him, but she was not. He took her beauty. Riches vanished before the very eyes of the bride.

Be sure of this: *In the abundance of the good and the gifts which God gives us, we take pleasure in looking at ourselves.*

But then comes the hour when the bride sees that she is beautiful only when it is the beauty *of her Groom.* She must learn when the beauty which is Christ is gone, whatever beauty is left to her is frightful indeed.

In her early relationship the girl would not have followed her lover into the desert or wherever He went. She would have been in fear of spoiling her beauty and losing her jewels. Oh, He would not have her beauty, her gifts, the capacities to spoil her. *He takes away that beauty.* Why? For a beauty more glorious—the beauty of the Groom. He cares not what appearance she is left with when her own beauty is gone.

In this season the Lord is taking away the ornaments, the gifts, the favor. It seems that He came first and took away graces, gifts and favors, that is, love which could be sensed and be pursued. Yes, these departed first. What He gave suddenly or by degree, He now takes away—suddenly or by degree.

Perhaps at this point the believer is not so concerned about the loss or riches, but about the disfavor of his Lord. So distraught by a feeling of unworthiness, the believer would not utter the prayer, "Lord, give me back what you gave me before." This believer knows that he does not deserve a positive answer to this prayer. All the Christian can do now is look at his Lord and suffer. The silence is interrupted only by tears, and yet the Christian feels that even his tears may be offending the Lord. He would gladly give up everything and never touch the gifts again, if only he knew he would not offend his Lord. Some such Christians may throw themselves into a thousand postures to appease their God, only to wake up one day and realize that this, too, is displeasing.

When finally the Lord *does* come back, after the Christian is so keenly aware of his weaknesses, his sin and his low estate, he can hardly believe that the Lord has come back.

Be sure, though, when the Lord returns, He is *not* going to return all the former riches. Now, however, the Christian *is no longer the least bit concerned about this!* He is simply content to cherish this period of time with his well-beloved.

There is a strange paradox here, though. If the Lord's presence stays for a long time with the dear believer, he will once more slip into forgetfulness; that is, he will forget the difficult times. His sense of his own wretchedness will disappear; he will feed once more upon the caresses and love of his Lord. Chances are, then, if the Lord does return bearing His riches, and remains for a good period of time . . . He will almost surely *depart again!*

If you are wondering whether you should be a weak Christian or a strong Christian, the answer is, *neither* will do you any good. If you are a weak Christian, then the last things are so difficult to let go, and the stripping takes so long. If you are a strong Christian, then you will find yourself struggling constantly, although you might be sooner finished because you will be exhausted sooner.

One day you will look back upon the Lord's stripping of things in your life and be astonished at His great love and the genius by which he did it. The soul is so full of itself, the Christian so taken up with self-love, if the Lord did not deal with us thusly, there would be no true progress at all.

Perhaps you will ask, "If the gifts of God are so distracting, why does He give them to us?"

He gives gifts to us out of his excellent goodness, draws the soul from sin by them, draws the believer from attachments to other things in creation, and uses them to turn the believer back to Him. If He did not give us His gifts, His riches, and His blessings, the soul would be—and remain forever—a criminal.

But, having been won with His gifts which He so graciously bestows, we do not realize that we are such wretched things, nor do we see that we are so wrapped in self-admiration. We turn our attention away from our Lord to the gifts. From giver to gift we travel. Self-love is a deeply rooted thing in all of us. The Lord's gifts only serve to increase self-love. They perhaps will take us from the love of the *world* and the love of *other things*, and even *to* a love of God; but they do *not* affect, *in any way*, our love and charm for *ourselves*.

The believer appropriates God's gifts to his self-love. Perhaps he is also growing too familiar with the Lord, forgetting the slavery out of which he was delivered, and a thousand more things.

Then why does the Lord not immediately deliver us? The answer lies wholly within the Lord alone, and if you ask that question and are offended because you receive no answer, then you might as well not make the journey. If knowing answers to such questions is absolutely necessary to you, then forget the journey. You will never make it, for this is a journey of unknowables—of unanswered questions, enigmas, incomprehensibles, and most of all, things unfair.

The Christian is now in a place where the divine gifts of the Lord have been stripped away. We see that he is recognizing his self-love, and he is beginning to realize that he is not as rich as he previously had thought he was. He sees that he has had a higher regard for himself than he *ever* realized—and that richness belongs to the Groom alone, not to the bride. He realizes he has made wrong use of those things which the Lord has given him and tells the Lord that he will be delighted if the Lord *never* gives them back! He requests only that he be rich with the riches of Christ.

For some Christians there may even be gladness at the loss of the gifts of God.

Why? Because the Christian feels that he has been relieved of a great deal of that which had encumbered him. He is now lightly equipped for spiritual progress.

Little by little we see this Christian being stripped. It is a thing of degrees. He does not care for his losses because serving the Lord is no longer one of his great priorities. He will seek to be pleasing to the Lord without ornaments, gifts and service.

The Christian is hoping now only for a peaceful state of affairs. It is mine to tell you that the peaceful state of affairs may not last. The Lord may come yet to strip away more. Even the garments. And if there *is* a further stripping, the poor soul knows not quite what to do.

"Alas," the believer cries, "I have lost all your riches which You gave me, your gifts, and even your sweet love. But at least I was able to perform some few external acts of virtue, some small acts of charity. Will You leave me now naked? If I lose my garments and am found naked, this will bring reproach even to You, O Lord. Shall You then consent to such a loss?"

Consent He does, indeed!

You *still* do not know your own self. You believe that your garments are your own and that you can make use of them as you wish. But the Lord would say to you, "What you are really saying is, 'Lord, I gained these garments at great cost by the things I did for You, the labors for which You rewarded me.' "

Lose them, dear soul.

The soul will do everything to keep the garments, but there will be more stripping; and this stripping, too, will come little by little.

The Christian may find himself now no longer interested in anything. There is no interest in works of charity, and certainly no power to perform them. Before there may have been *disgust*. And there may have been *pain*. But now there is only *impotence*.

The Christian begins to lose his remembrance of the fairer and finer days. Again the poor Christian, once more watching yet further loss, believes these losses are the result of some great fault within him. He really knows nothing to say in the presence of his God. Little by little he realizes that he has nothing of his own—absolutely nothing—and that everything belongs to the Bridegroom. Little by little there is coming that total distrust of self, and little by little—degree by degree—the love of self is dying.

Ah, but it is one thing to *cease* from self-love; it is another thing to *hate* yourself. The Christian remembers when he thought that this matter of having all things stripped away was a small thing. But today he sees himself as one who was *never* worthy (not before, not now, not ever). He sees that he has never been in the past, and will never be in the future, worthy of wearing the glorious, white wedding garment. The Christian is at last exposed for what he is—naked. Ashamed of this fact, he is devastated. He hardly dares walk into the Lord's presence.

"At least," he thinks, "if only my nakedness could be a private, and not a public, thing." Admiration is gone now. The world is not only paying no attention to this believer (or is shocked at his impotence) but the world is forgetting him.

What an incredible fall this one has experienced! The Christian is doubly confused because he knows he has deserved everything that has happened to him. He has some hope of being clothed again, but he knows not what to do to bring it to pass.

Here, then, is the Christian who once believed himself far advanced in the maturity of things spiritual, even coming to a point of perfection in the matter of service. Now he can hardly stand to remember the days when such thoughts were in his mind. But those were the days when the garments concealed the true person. Now there is nothing.

So what are we seeing here? A Lord who has stripped away everything, and who would turn even beauty to ugliness . . . and then destroy the ugliness. Surely this is the end! But no, it is not.

At this point, the Christian has submitted to the stripping of gifts, graces, favors, the desire for service, the capacity to do good, to fast, to help his neighbor. He has lost everything except that which is *divine*. Will even this be called upon?

It is a dreadful thing to be in a state where one is naked of the gifts *and* graces of God. No one who has not experienced it would believe it.

What am I saying? The Christian loses virtue as virtue. He will find it again only as it is Jesus Christ. It seems the soul has now lost everything—that is, everything but the Lord's beauty.

It is difficult to explain; the believer who has suffered all these things until now and allowed them to be lost has, nonetheless, been very *mindful* that it is *he* who has allowed these things to pass. He has faced rebellion on occasion, but he has not rebelled. He has lost all sense of the Lord, but he has not rebelled against the Lord. As in the Song of Songs, he can say,

> *The watchmen found me and*
> *wounded me.*

This Christian has seen corruption in himself the way Job has seen it. He has felt like crying out as did Job, "Oh, that I might hide myself in hell until the anger of God is past." The soul has been overwhelmed with the purity of God. He has seen the smallest mote of imperfection as an enormous sin. And yet it is a *general* sense of his imperfections. It is not particular faults that are weighing him down; it is a sense of his *total* unworthiness. There is just the possibility that despite all the faults he might be capable of enumerating, his motives and his heart were never so pure.

Then what fault is there here? Only this: The Christian's *relationship* to his Lord is turned toward his own well-being.

Has he arrived at some state of perfection? Not at all. What *is* his relationship to sin? Often what he has done, he only recognizes as sin *after* he has done it; and at that moment he cries out to the Lord for help and for forgiveness.

But there is coming into the experience of the believer now a sense of hating his own soul. He is beginning to hate it because he is beginning to *know* it. All knowledge in the world that a man might have and all that he might read and all the information he might acquire will never cause him to *hate* his own soul. To *hate* oneself is the *only* experience which gives the soul a knowledge of *the infinite depth of wretchedness*. And in that knowledge, that *spiritual* knowledge, is the only course to true purity. *Impurities pressed out by any other means are not removed, only hidden.*

The Lord begins now to search out those radical impurities. He is in search of things that are there because of a deep and invisible self-love.

Let us illustrate in this way. Here is a sponge full of all sorts of impurities, and you wash it. You cannot possibly make it clean within unless it is pressed. Washing will not remove it all. Only when it is squeezed does the inner storage of corruption and impurity come out. And this is what the Lord now does to the believer. The *most* hidden things are what God is now after.

The Christian thinks He is finding new sin in his life, but it is quite the contrary. What is being discovered is something unseen that has been there *all along*. It is discovered and *seen* now, only because it is being removed!

Nonetheless, the Christian will invariably believe that he has fallen into new depths of carnality and sinfulness. When that which has been so impure, so hidden, and so deep within for so long at last reaches the surface, the Christian thinks surely he has *just now* picked up these sins and impurities.

The Lord is not concerned about the inconvenience you suffer while beholding these horrible things as they come to the surface. He knows, as frightening as they are, there is no other way to deal with self-love. Until now, a deep and hidden love of self has been covered with beautiful garments. The *deeper* that self-love has sunk into your being—the more hidden it is—the more ruin it causes. Why? Because its mischief is not known, and all your external aspects look so noble.

The very *discovery* of these hidden things is in itself a purifying experience! The soul needs to discover what is inside. The self nature needs to see what it really is, and what it is like—right to the very bottom.

We should also know that many will look upon you with wonder because what you now consider to be great faults, they have always considered to be great strengths and virtues of the Christian life! They will also be sure that in your losing of them you are losing virtue itself.

Others may know your outward and superficial faults. Those faults which God seeks out in the inmost parts of the soul are matters which pass for perfections in the eyes of man. Prudence, wisdom, and a thousand other things, they would tell you to cherish dearly.

Many great souls have many great virtues. But the Christian of whom I am speaking now has none at all. All he has is weakness on weakness, impotence on impotence. Another believer may go forth on what he *sees*, and he subsists on things that are great. But this Christian moves, not by what he *has*, internally . . . but by what has been *removed from him, internally.*

He has lost all.

What other Christians do is admired; what this believer does is . . . failure. Everything this believer does is thwarted. Everything he touches he spoils. He succeeds at nothing and is approved in nothing. Where is the Lord taking him? To see all happiness in the Bridegroom and *nothing* in himself.

You could never believe, unless you experienced it, what human nature is capable of when it is left to itself. Sometimes I feel that our own nature, left to itself, is worse than all the devils.

But I do not mean to leave the impression here that this Christian, in this wretched state, is forsaken by God. Not at all. Never before has he been sustained so well by his Lord.

Nonetheless, the Christian is in a poor state of affairs, and the best thing that can happen to him is that God show *no* pity! When the Lord wishes to aid the progress of a believer, he lets that believer run even to death. And when there is respite, and the Christian rejoices once more in this life, that respite—and the life that is given—is given for reasons of the believer's weakness, lest he should lose all spirit.

As a runner who is running after his goal, the believer would never stop running, except there are times he must *rest* and receive *nourishment*. But both of these needs are because of his inherent weakness. There comes a time when something within the believer dies out. This comes at or near the end of the course. There is some sort of mysterious death that takes place within. It is as if the sun had disappeared from our hemisphere. It is no longer visible, but hidden in the sea. (We will see this state shortly.) This is a time when the Christian undergoes yet another kind of death . . . a time when he begins to realize how noisy he is inside.

It is interesting to note the state of this Christian in relationship to other believers—that is, to Christians who are (or appear to be) very advanced in their internal walk with the Lord.

The poor one sees these other believers all decked with so many spoils of victory. It is obvious that the Lord, the Bridegroom, has laid many ornaments upon these believers.

The desolate Christian admires these things so much, and sees himself in an abyss of nothing. Yet he has no desire to have all the beautiful things he sees before his eyes. For one thing, he feels too unworthy of them. He rejoices, though, to see that others are in favor with the Lord.

When the believer first started out on this long journey, he had a jealousy for the presence of God and wished to keep the Lord always with him. *Now* he is grateful when he feels the Lord is *not* looking at him, for he would not have the Lord look upon such a sight. The Christian has reached the point where he can see no good in his nakedness, his death, or this putrefaction . . . which he has newly discovered of himself.

The Lord has made this one naked, in order that the Lord Himself might be his clothing.

"Put on the Lord Jesus Christ."

He kills only that He Himself might be the believer's life.

"If we have died with Christ,
we shall rise with Him."

The Lord annihilates the Christian only to transform him into Himself.

The loss of personal virtue takes place only by degrees, as do all other losses. The end is something akin to utter despair; this believer not only has lost hope in his outward virtues, but even self-love has lost its power.

Prayer in this particular stage is very painful. In fact, it is not surprising that a Christian may not even be able to lay hold of prayer. There was a time when a sweet and profound calm was in prayer, and that calm *sustained* prayer. But God has withdrawn this. Prayer seems to be lost. The Christian finds himself the same as believers who have never practiced praying. There is one difference, though: he feels the pain of the loss.

This Christian, in this stage of his journey, might go astray from time to time; but it is usually a momentary thing, an *impetuous* thing. There is no satisfaction in it; instead there is only bitterness, and he withdraws as quickly as possible.

There *is* one other thing left, though!

There is something that every child of God has within him. It is a certain secret, a certain tranquil something within him, that comforts him even in his death and impotence. Whatever this element is, it is a thing deep in the inmost part of the believer, subtle yet very powerful. Now here is something so pure, so much Christian, that it would seem to be the ultimate end of that for which all the Christian religion is intended and the reward for all a believer's labors. What indeed does the follower of the Lord desire except to have this testimony in his inmost being: the testimony that he is a child of God. All spirituality centers in this simple experience. Ah, but even *this* must be *given up*. Just as all other things have been required, so this, also!

At last we have come to that which truly works death in the believer! You see, it matters not what wretchedness the soul experiences, if that certain *something* is still there. In fact, the thing most needful to bring about death will not come as long as that deep, almost imperceptible sense is present.

This is a time of great fear. There can be agony in the heart. In fact, it seems the only life the heart has left in it is but to tell of the death that it is in.

It is this imperceptible support and the experience of wretchedness that follows *these* two things, which cause death.

There is one thing needed above all else at this time, and that is that the believer be faithful. This is a hard time and a time of nakedness. The Christian will turn anywhere for comfort and refreshment. He is incapable of virtually any Christian action, and is in great need of solace.

And if you are a Christian who meets such a one and he is looking for comfort or guidance, what can you do? Be careful to do nothing that would soothe or take away the Christian's newfound discovery of his great imperfection. Refresh him with love, with charity, and with innocent things. Hold in your mind that this person you are dealing with feels that he has little control over his interior circumstances. To try to force him back to a more normal situation could very well ruin his health, his mind, and his interior life. Do not be severe, but deal as with a child. [1]

Nonetheless, please note that what I am saying here I apply only to those in this particular stage, and this stage alone.

Now, why is it the Lord has taken away even the element of internal sense? It is to deliver this sense, spiritual intuition, out of an imperfect operation and into yet a deeper interior. And how is the Lord making the person more perfect in this deeper interior? By weaning him of trust in, and even a perception of, his outward senses. He now bids the believer inwardly in a way so gentle that the cost of moving in that direction is scarcely

---

1 Editor's note: Guyon's advice here is very wise. In my entire ministry I have only met one or two Christians in this state of affairs. The only advice I have ever been able to give them, other than helping them understand the situation they are in, is to suggest: (1) they cry a lot and (2) that they listen to a lot of comforting Christian music! G.E.

recognized, even when it means that he is to lose all things.

At this time, the Lord sometimes does something quite paradoxical. He will sometimes reawaken the outward senses. Yet all things work together for them that love God and are *called* to *His* purpose. Once more the Christian learns a great distrust in himself, no matter what his state. And if friends do not understand what is going on, the soul simply replies,

> "Do not look upon me for reasons that
> I am black, for it is the sun that has
> made me so unsightly."

And so we come to the next stage in the Christian's plunge toward the sea, which is his burial.

7

The torrential river has now come through all imaginable roarings and tossings. It has been hurled against rocks. It has tumbled from one rock to another, from one level to another. But it has always been in full view; never has it been swallowed up from sight. At this point it begins to plunge into deep caverns. It is for a long time invisible. Perhaps we will see this river for a little while, only to watch it disappear again into some deep gulf. Out of sight, if falls from abyss to abyss.

(Eventually it will fall into the abyss of the sea, and there, losing itself, never to find itself again, it will have become part of the sea itself.)

After many deaths and after ever increasing severities, the believer expires at length in the arms of Love, but *without ever perceiving* that he rests within these arms.

And what are we speaking of here? This person, personified in the experience of the river, now simply and very subtly loses all desire, inclination and choices. The nearer this torrent draws to death, the weaker it becomes. Although death was inevitable, as long as life was there, there was some hope; but now there is hope no longer. The torrent falls beneath the earth and is seen no more.

The believer has known great precipices from which he has fallen; but now he falls, not from a precipice, but into some unseen abyss. Now has come a misery from which there is no day of deliverance. Upon first entering this abyss it does not appear to be so great. The further the believer plunges into it, though, the more dreadful this place is found to be.

You see, after a man expires, he is still among the living. He is dead, but he has not been put away. So here we see a soul who still bears some semblance of life. It is a slight bit of body heat still left in the corpse.

What am I saying here?

The soul still attempts to worship and pray. But as the abyss deepens, these are soon left behind. He must lose God, or at least it will appear so to him. For him there is almost a certainty that he has lost his Lord, not for a period of months or years, but that he has lost his Lord whom he has known throughout his life . . . *forever!*

Once he was afraid of the world; now the world is afraid of him! As to his fellow believers, there is a certain respect given by the living to those who are about to be interred. They are, after all, about to cast this poor one into the earth, there to be thought of no more.

If the human body could see what was happening to it when it was buried, it would feel a great deal of stress. Well, the soul *can* see all this, and is sometimes terrified. But there is nothing it can do.

The believer suffers himself to be buried and covered with the earth. At this point this devotee begins to be horrified at himself, the reason being that God has obviously cast him off so far that it seems as though the Lord has certainly abandoned him forever. What then can this one do? He must have patience and simply lie in the sepulchre.

The soul is now there and sees that there is very little likelihood of ever getting out; he must remain in this state forever. And further, this devotee truly believes that *here* is a fitting place for him. The world speaks no longer of this one and regards him as nothing more than a corpse that has lost the life of grace and is fit for nothing. The soul bears this state patiently. But alas, this state is sweet when compared with what is to follow.

Now the soul must *rot*.

Before, the believer was tried by weakness and fainting. But the believer has now seen the depth of his corruption. This believer has reached a state where he sees the entire sweep of all that has happened to him. The troubles, scorns, contradictions, everything *cease* to affect this one. Even reflection on the passion of the sufferings of the Son of God does not touch him.

There is no remedy for this state. It simply must be passed through.

Perhaps the believer would now say, "I could endure this gradual return to dust if only God would not look upon me. What sorrow must my state cause Him!" His delight is that perhaps the Lord has so turned in disfavor from him that at least he is spared knowing that the Lord is watching his decay.

And will this state of decay last but a short time? Alas, it is quite the opposite. It will last several years and go on, continually increasing, until (toward the end) there is no longer the rotting away but the turning to dust. And dust returns to dust and ashes to ashes.

The poor river, now plunged into an abyss,

drops even deeper and deeper, until there is an end of all good resolutions and austerity.

Compare now the difference between the state of this torrential river when it was flowing from the source, flowing pleasantly over the plains and down the rills. And now see its frightening plunge.

And yet, *this* was its destiny.

A very interesting thing happens about this time. The soul begins to become accustomed to this situation. It stays *quite without hope* with no thought of escaping. It is totally incapable of relieving the situation. The hidden motives of the heart are being annihilated and becoming dust. At least, annihilation of the dark things of the self has *begun*.

Now the corpse is nothing but ashes; the soul no longer suffers from its surroundings. It has become naturalized to this strange and quite indescribable environment.

The believer ceases to look at anything, and is like a person who is no more and who will never be again. Previously this Christian was horrified at his nature. *Now* there is no reaction to it. Formerly, he came with dread to communion, with fear of dishonoring God. Now he seems to approach it as a matter of course. There is no longer any sense, either of that which brings pain or that which brings pleasure. The ashes rest in some kind of peace, but a peace without hope; ashes have no hope. Even when the soul was aware of its rotting away, it was at least that—*still* aware. Now it has gone through that state; and nothing, either within or without, affects it any longer.

At length, in this Christian who is being reduced to a nonentity, there is found in his ashes a germ of immortality. Preserved underneath it all is, like a germ, something that will, in due time, live. But be sure, the devotee is not aware of this. He has no thought of being ever revived or resuscitated.

Is there faithfulness in this one? Only faithfulness in allowing himself to be buried, crushed; no more faithfulness than a dead person!

If you would perfume yourself that you might not stink in corruption, do it not, poor soul. Leave yourself just where you are. Submit. To have come so far and to seek now to come out of this state by applying sweet balm is to do yourself mischief. The Lord is bearing with you; why should you not bear with yourself?

And if another Christian is seeking to help the believer who is in this state of affairs, what should be his course? It is my opinion that you should do very little to relieve such a person. Sustain him only in the *preservation of the sanity of his mind,* since otherwise he might be destroyed by his own distress. There is pain here that goes to the very marrow of the bones. Other pains were more external; this has penetrated deeply. Do not show pity to this person. Leave him in the state which he feels he is apparently in, because—however he looks upon it—to God it is a state most pleasing. From those ashes is born a new life.

The one who has been reduced to nothingness ought not to wish to get out of this state or to live as he did formerly. He should continue looking back upon that state as something that no longer is.

And now, at last, the swiftly running river plunges into the sea and loses itself there, never again to find itself. It has become one and the same with the sea.

Now something will take place. Little by little this dead thing begins to feel, and yet what it experiences is without feeling. By degree the ashes are reviving and taking on a new life. Nonetheless, this process is very gradual. To the one in whose life it is happening, it is more like a dream or a delightful vision. You could liken it this way: There are ashes, and the ashes are forming a worm; and that worm is taking life by degrees.

We are now coming to the last stage, but it is only the *beginning* of that last stage. The *beginning*, no more than a beginning, of the truly interior life. The strata within this last stage are without number. And where the soul may advance to is without limit. The swirling river can go further and further into the sea and take more and more of the quality of the sea, simply by dwelling longer within that sea.

8

Let a grain of wheat reveal some of the elements of your spiritual life.

First, the chaff is separated from the grain. This is an example of your conversion and separation from sin. After the grain has been separated, it must be ground by trials and by the cross. The grain is ground until it is reduced to flour. The process, however, is far from finished. The flour is course and must have foreign matter removed from it.

The flour is kneaded and made into pastry. The flour appears dark as it is kneaded, but the kneading is essential for the flour to be made into pastry. The pastry, in turn, must be put into the fire. After the pastry is baked, it is destined for the king's delight. The king not only looks upon the pastry with delight, he partakes of it.

This comparison shows you some of the different aspects of your spiritual journey. It shows you the difference between union with God and transformation.

To be transformed you must lose all your own properties so that you might partake more deeply of God's nature. Not many people come to this place. For this reason, people do not talk much about the cross and transformation. We cannot speak well upon subjects we know little about.

When one loses himself in God, he will seem very ordinary. There is nothing that externally distinguishes this one from others . . . except, of course, his freedom.

This freedom often scandalizes people who see nothing more than what they themselves have experienced. They suppose that anything they themselves have not experienced must be *bad*. But the freedom they condemn (a simple freedom and an innocent freedom) is a greater holiness than what is usually considered to be holy! A small action, accomplished through God's nature working in a believer, is more acceptable to God than many heroic actions done in man's own strength.

Activity which comes from God rather than

from the strength of man is rare and precious. Believers who come to this place in their spiritual life are satisfied with what they do from moment to moment and do not need to seek after what the world considers great things.

God chooses to hide the people who know Him well. He hides them under the cover of an ordinary life. They are His prized ones and are known to Him alone. God flows through these individuals because they have come to know their Lord within.

The treasure is not revealed until the treasure is needed. Nonetheless, God, working through such a one, is often noticed by others.

Not all these people are unknown, and people who do noticeable things are not always doing such works from their own strength.

Your Lord draws people to these believers, and they are often able to communicate life to others. They naturally win others over to Jesus Christ.

Some, though, however angelic in appearance they seem, are very far from this state. This is a walk which usually takes a long time to enter into fully. (God in His sovereignty may speed up the process, but such cases are very rare.) His work in us is designed to take a lifetime.

Part of being totally abandoned to Him means one does not evaluate how he is being used by God. As Christ becomes rooted in a believer more deeply, that one is less self-conscious about his relationship to God.

Continue growing. Let your spirit be enlarged to greater and greater degrees. God can enlarge your spirit daily. You will be expanded in Him like the torrent. Let yourself be carried further and further into the sea. You will never exhaust your understanding of how you dwell in God and how God dwells in you.

The process of losing oneself in God happens in different degrees in different people. Every person can be completely full. But some have larger capacities than others. A cup and a pitcher can both be full of water, but each holds different amounts. Every person has his own capacity to receive the fullness of God. The wonderful thing is that God is able to enlarge this capacity day by day.

The more you live by inward grace, the larger your spirit grows, without effort on your part. Allow His nature to dwell more fully within you. To the same degree that He enlarges you, He fills you. It is the same with air. A small room is full of air, but a larger room has even more. Enlarge the room and there is even more air in it. In the same way (without becoming aware of any change) your spirit expands and increases. How does this happen? By learning to die daily. The hard thing is that one's oldness naturally resists death.

How does one grow and die at the same time? This is not a contradiction. Your unique personality, that is your soul, is small and limited. God needs to purify you and to alter you in order for you to receive His gifts.

Your spirit, however, is eternal and can continually expand. You can experience God in ever-increasing ways. Your soul's own desires, as good as they may be, also stand in the way of letting this expansion happen. The part that stands in the way is the part that must die—not your unique personality. You must let go of your old nature so that you might lose yourself more deeply in God. Your ability to grow in Him is limitless.

9

As a torrent empties into the sea, its waters can be distinguished from the sea for quite a long time, but gradually the waters of this river mix with the sea completely. Likewise, your transformation will not happen overnight; but little by little, degree by degree, you lose your own life.

The only thing that is left of a body that has completely decayed is dust and ashes. However, as one dies to his old ways he does not lose all the uniqueness that makes him who he is. Actually, it is quite the opposite. Only through this death process will you be truly set free to be who you really are.

All that has taken place in one's life up until now has been the stripping and cleaning of the soulish nature. All of us need this stripping in order to receive the work of God within us.

As the torrent flows into the sea, its own shape is lost. In a similar manner, you must part with some element of your natural disposition in order that the nature of God might live more fully within you. When you live by His nature, His life, it is His life which sustains you.

The torrent, once emptied into the sea, now has all the treasure of the sea. The more the torrent empties into the sea, the more full and more glorious the torrent becomes.

In this experience of death, the believer begins to come back to life. Explore this new life, for it is like nothing you have ever known before.

Should you discover this life you will truly say:

> "Those who were in darkness have seen
> a great light, and to them that sat in the
> region of the shadow of death has the day
> arisen." (Isaiah 9:2)

Ezekiel foreshadows this resurrection when he sees the dry bones become flesh by degrees.

Be amazed to find a secret force beginning to possess you. Your ashes will begin to revive.

A new country beckons to you. When you were in the grave the only thing that you could do was to quietly stay there. But now you can experience a most pleasant surprise. Do not be afraid to believe what is happening.

At this point you may say, "Perhaps the sun has found a small hole in the tomb to shine one of its rays through, but night will no doubt fall again."

Dear believer, be delighted to feel a strong and secret power taking hold of you. You will have received a new life. Believe.

Can you lose this state? Of course. But you would have to launch a major rebellion to do so.

This new life is not like the old one. Here is "life in God" (Colossians 3:3). Here is His life. You no longer live but Christ lives and acts and works within you (Galatians 2:20).

Resurrection life expands degree by degree so that you will grow in the growth of God. Richness flows from His riches within you. He is the love by which you will now love.

At this point you begin to see that all you did before, no matter how great, was your own doing. You will no longer be doing anything of yourself. You will be possessed by a new life. Take this new life and lose it in God. Live with the life of God. And since He Himself is Life, you cannot want for anything more.

What gain has been made compared to the little that has been lost! You will have lost "the creature" in order to gain "the Creator." You will have lost your nothingness in order to gain all things. You will be boundless, for you will have inherited God! Your capacity to experience His life will grow just a little more. Everything that you once had, and lost, will return to you in God.

Please note that as one is stripped, degree by degree, so now he is enriched and called back to life, degree by degree. The more he lost, the more he will gain. Be like the torrent which empties into the sea. The torrent expands to explore the boundless limits of its new home.

Do not try to attain to this experience. Let this oneness grow from His nature, which is at work within you. As He works in you, you will become flexible and agreeable to whatever circumstances God allows in your life. Count whatever God brings to you as good. Feast times and times of famine will become the same to you. All circumstances are equal; the believer sees God behind all things.

The divine life within will feel natural to you as you grow accustomed to it. Learn to give yourself up to the ways of this new life. Let there be no struggle.

A momentary unfaithfulness will cause you to act apart from God. This does not mean that you have fallen out of your position in God. You have simply missed the gentle moving of God in your spirit which causes you to be in complete oneness with the Lord.

You do not have to think about how to find God or worry about your thoughts wandering away from Him; you dwell within God. No need to spend time trying to locate your God, for He is your indwelling and your circumstances. Before, it was necessary to practice virtue in order to do good works. Now your actions have their origin in God.

If a person were completely surrounded by the sea, one place in the sea would not be more suitable or profitable than another part of the sea . . . for the purpose of experiencing the sea. So it will be with you and your Lord. Let the life within you carry you along. That is enough.

Should you do anything? Simply do what you are prompted to do by an indwelling Lord. Embrace the circumstances which are brought to you to experience. A constant and unchangeable peace can be yours, no matter what the circumstances.

10

How does your life, once you have entered this way, differ from your life when it was entirely lived in the flesh? Before, it was your human nature that prompted you. Now it should be that you live your life in a peaceful and satisfied manner and do the things that are required of you.

God alone should be your guide. When it appears there is "something" for you to give up, then give up your will to God; then your will shall no longer rule you, for you will have given it over to God. Desires that do not spring forth from His will need not hold power over you. Let them fade away. As you live from your spirit, you should begin to lose the inclinations and biases and contrary feelings that lead you astray. The torrent no longer goes its own way.

What is this wonderful contentment that fills the heart? God Himself. Nothing else satisfies you so completely. Put away all views of your own—*no matter how insightful.*

Nothing should overshadow God's work within you—neither knowledge nor intelligence nor even human love. Something has actually died within you. Part of your past ways are gone. You now experience "a lack of feeling," but it will be very different from what you knew in the grave. There you were deprived of life—separated from the world with all the indifference of a person who is dead. But your Lord will bring you above that condition. You will not feel deprived. How can one feel deprived of that which he does not miss? Death is something that you recoil from in fear and disgust. Life, on the other hand, is glorious. The believer is raised up and is given life. This life is not maintained through the senses but flows from the fountain of eternal life. This eternal life is Christ within you.

Compare life to death. When you die, you feel the separation of yourself from your body. After the soul separates from the body you no longer feel any physical sensation—you are dead and separated from your environment.

When you are raised up you have new life within you. When God resurrects you from the dead you will experience God being the Spirit of your spirit and the Life of your life. He becomes the very center of your life and your source of life. You should then live, act and walk from the life of God within you.

When you experience some delight apart from God, or when you try to retire in order to find God, or when you focus on trials and pain, you will not be walking in His life. Your spirit should be so entwined with God's Spirit that you will not experience Him as someone separate and distinct, but only as someone who is deeply joined with you. He can become more active within you than you are yourself.

If a person could live without eating, he probably would. Eating or not eating would be the same because whether he ate or not, he would still feel full. This experience is like unto death. But there is some difference. When you are sick or near death, your lack of appetite comes from illness. In this case, however, it will be from being too full. If a person lived on air, he would be full without even knowing how he became full. Just breathing would make him full. He would not be empty or unable to eat—it just would not be necessary for him to eat. The air he breathed would naturally sustain him.

Realize that when you are so enveloped and sustained by God, you are in what is truly your natural environment. You breathe in the atmosphere that you were made for. A new kind of peace will come to you. In the grave your peace was still and quiet—appropriate to the state of burial and rest that you were in. It is the kind of peace that a dead man would feel in the middle of a great storm at sea.

There is a place high above the waves of the turbulent sea where you are able to observe the fury of the stormy sea. Your vantage point is high upon the mountain. On the mountain nothing will be able to touch you.

This experience can be compared to living at the bottom of the ocean where, during the turbulent storms, only the surface of the ocean experiences the stormy weather. Deep below it is tranquil. The outward senses may suffer pain, but the deepest parts of the spirit dwell in undisturbed rest.

Note that you will not always be faithful. There are times when you will go back to your old ways of doing things. The possibility exists, nonetheless, for you to make great advances in God. A person falling into a bottomless sea could fall forever only to discover deeper and more beautiful treasures. So it is with one's plunge into God.

11

What must you do to be faithful to God? Nothing. Less than nothing: Let God alone be your life! Allow only God to move you. Do not resist Him. Continue to live by the natural flow of His life within you. Live in the present moment and let each event unfold without adding or subtracting from it. Learn to be led by the instinctive impressions of the life of God within you. Your Lord will make your way for you. Let Him also carry out all that He requires of you. Your task is but to simply dwell in this state.

When you begin to act out of your own strength, you will become unfaithful to the divine life within you. Don't let dependence on your strength become a habit. Allow yourself to die without looking for a rescue.

A person who is dying wishes to be done with anything that might prolong his agony. He has no use for anything that might help him—he is resigned to his death. After he dies, nothing has any effect on him.

When the right time has come for you to be stripped of your life, submit to it.

You will be able to possess all things *without* owning them. All that is left is easy: Do God's pleasure, God's way, by God's strength.

Faithfulness is not just "doing nothing." Faithfulness is acting only from His life. In this state one has no inclination for things to go one's own way, but desires only God's way. Actions will spring from a different source.

Do not think that at this juncture in your sojourn you will commit no faults. You will. And you will see them more clearly than ever. The faults that you commit will probably not be gross sins, but subtle driftings. You will be able to more clearly see your smallest shortcomings. Do not let these imperfections cause you to be brought into a sense of guilt. And do nothing to get rid of these faults.

You will sense a cloud of dust, like a film, settling over you when you commit a fault. Do nothing to try to clear this cloud out of the way. Such efforts are useless. Such efforts will only make it take longer for you to be restored to normal. Being overly concerned with your faults is worse for your spiritual condition than the fault itself.

At these times you should not feel you need "to return to God." For if you say you must return, it suggests that you have become alienated from the Lord. Not so. You dwell in God. Simply *remain* in Him. Sometimes there will be cloudiness in this experience: but you should not try to move the clouds yourself. Let the sun do that.

Looking at yourself too much slows down your journey. The longer you continue to gaze at yourself the more you will lose. You cannot see yourself as God sees you. When self-centered thoughts come, let them pass without holding on to them. Little by little they will go away.

As the Christian leaves the tomb of death, he will experience desires coming forth more from Jesus Christ than from himself. He will no longer live by a prescribed set of actions which he has been told he is supposed to follow.

Let *Him* be your rules to live by! You will find that the nature of Christ comes forth from deep within you without effort. The Christian's nature grows naturally from the Lord's Spirit within his spirit.

Your treasure is God alone. Draw your life from His life for He is eternal. Clothe yourself with Jesus Christ. Allow Him to act and speak within you. Let *Him* initiate all your actions. Yield to Him and take no action at all! Rest as He prompts you.

Do you see the immeasurable progress you can make? The more experience you have, the better able you are to discern His life within you.

12

Yielding completely to Christ takes much longer than one might think. And it is not easy. The believer should not fool himself into thinking that he has arrived or that arrival can come quickly. Even the most spiritually mature have fallen into this mistake.

The reason many of those who follow the Lord do not advance very far is because back in the beginning they had not allowed themselves to be stripped. Or, just as wrong, they had tried to accomplish this stripping by themselves. You cannot strip yourself. As much as you wish to follow the Lord, and as much as you wish to be stripped, your own efforts to do so will only make you religious and hard or extremely confused. God will come and He will strip you.

What place does prayer hold in the life of the pilgrim at this point? If there is any enjoyment in any kind of prayer, continue it. But if there is none, then be willing to lay prayer down. Do not lay down anything that has been helpful to you spiritually. Do so only when it becomes totally distasteful, difficult, and unproductive.

You must understand that the way of the cross—this way of allowing yourself to be completely emptied—is one that will be full of dryness for you. There is difficulty, there is pain and there is weariness. The beginning of your spiritual journey is glorious, beautiful and rich. Do not confuse the beginning with the end or the middle. They so often have little in common and bear no similarity to one another. There are parts of the journey that are spiritual, but they can also be so difficult and so dry that the word "spiritual" seems to not even apply.

How fortunate, how blessed is the believer who can find someone along the way who will help him understand these things and show him that "spiritual" includes the dry, the desolate, and even the sense of being forsaken.

13

What are the imprints that the Lord will leave on this journeying Christian (the torrent), rushing into the vast ocean?

The process involved in the transformation of the life of the believer begins at the *very moment* he yields himself to the Lord. As this process continues, he will make many mistakes and there will be many faults. As the believer matures, he will move from looking at his faults to simply having a deep knowing within him that his desire is to be conformed to the image of his Lord. The believer will come to *desire* the work of the *cross* within him.

Later, though, even this desire to know the cross may seem to disappear. Actually, this desire to know the cross does not so much disappear as it simply goes down into the deep subterranean parts of his being. There is a secret and *hidden* longing for the cross. This longing is almost imperceptible, and goes deeper and deeper into the being of the believer. Let the cross work in you, and especially let it work in the most secret and inmost parts of your being. Let the cross work its singleness of purpose in the most hidden *motives* of your soul.

* * *

When speaking of "impressions" of the spirit or "inclinations" of an indwelling Lord, please understand: These do not come to you from the external. They come from within. From within is where they originate. Such promptings of the spirit work their way from the inside . . . outward; from deep within your spirit they finally come to your mind. This is the Lord welling up in you; this becomes the natural way of the believer's spiritual course. Here is the true *wellspring* of your spiritual being. Jesus Christ always reveals Himself from within you. You will live from Him. Search for Him on the outside, and you will never find Him.

The human body does all of its most important life-sustaining actions naturally and automatically. You do not have to think about breathing. So it must become in the development of the believer that the nudgings of the spirit within you become both natural and (virtually) imperceptible.

As Christ grows within you, you will be transformed into His likeness. Perhaps you will recognize that this is exactly the way the Lord Himself related to His Father.

14

At this point, what role does the cross play in the life of the seeking believer? As he grows strong with the strength of His Lord, the believer discovers that he is given a heavier and heavier cross by His Lord. He learns to bear this cross with the Lord's strength, not his own.

Up until now, there will have been somewhat a delight in the cross, but no more. The seeking soul will allow the cross to come for one reason: because it pleases God. Like everything else, the cross becomes a means of encountering the Lord Himself.

The cross will become for you a deep way of experiencing your Lord. Eventually there will come a point when the cross will not even be viewed as "the cross." It simply becomes another means of knowing Christ.

God's nature becomes more fully manifest in the believer through the cross, and the Christian grows more intimately acquainted with His Lord by encountering that cross. Perhaps at this point you will be able to look back and remember your early walk with the Lord. Remember? At first being a Christian was a joyful thing. *Then* you learned about the cross. And then the cross became very important to you.

The cross will work the work of God in you. But now the work of God will bring the cross to you, and the cross will bring the Lord Himself to you.

The believer must always be able to see God in all his circumstances. He must see this: that the coming of the cross is really something that comes from the Lord's hand. Not from man, not from circumstances, but from Him. Each moment of life, no matter what that moment holds, will be a moment when more of your Lord is being brought to you.

There are those who speak of visions, ecstasy, ravishments and revelations. They speak of much going on within themselves. But the believer who has known the cross to the point that the cross has become Christ Himself does not speak of visions or ecstasies or revelations. He walks by a simple and pure faith. He see God and God only. And when this sojourner looks out of his own eyes, he sees things as though he were looking through the eyes of God. He sees his own life, he sees his surrounding circumstances, he sees other believers, he sees friends and enemies, he sees principalities and powers, he sees the whole course of the pageantry of history itself through the eyes of God . . . and is content.

The more the Lord has worked His cross into the life of a believer, strangely enough, the more ordinary he seems to become. Outward spiritual expressions are not his strong points. It is only as you get to know him better, or as God gives you eyes to see, that you realize this person truly is extraordinary.

15

These dealings of God in your life lead you to true freedom. This freedom, however, does not lead you into irresponsibility. You will still fulfill your required duties. This freedom will bring you to doing the things that God desires of you. After all, you have discovered you are in God.

The only one who has been raised from the dead is one whose actions and energies are *of life*. If someone has been resurrected but continues without life, then where is his resurrection? A believer who has truly tasted death and has been restored should have, as one of the elements of his new life, the ability to do that which he was able to do before he died. Of course, there will be an element of a difference. Now he will do those things in God and by God, not by means of his own strength. This is not something that can be explained; it is not something that any book can teach. This is something that has to be experienced under the crucible of the cross; it comes *only* out of the experience of death.

Lazarus came back to his everyday life after he was raised from the dead. And even the Lord Jesus Christ after His resurrection was pleased to eat, drink and talk with men. If one is still bound and cannot pray, and if there are still the deep fears, deep struggles of guilt, and so many other things that go with our nature, then that person has not yet been raised from death. When you are restored, you are not only restored but—spiritually speaking—you are restored manifold over.

There is a beautiful example of this in the book of Job. Job is a mirror of a believer's entire spiritual journey. God stripped him of all of his worldly goods, and then God stripped him of his children. His *worldly goods* represent Job's *gifts*; his *children* represent Job's good works. Then God took Job's health, which is a symbol of Job's outward *virtues*.

Job was accused of sinning. He was accused of not resigning himself to the will of God. His friends told him he was being justly punished. In their eyes it was obvious that there must have been some terrible thing that Job had done, some sin that caused all of this woe. But after Job had suffered nearly to the point of death, God restored him. Yet Job was not exactly the same as he had been previously.

So also will be the resurrection of the believer. Everything is more or less given back to him, and yet so much has changed. The believer is no longer attached to *things* as he was before. He does not use *things* as once he did. Everything is done in God. Things are used as they are needed. He will not possess them as he formerly did, and that is a great place to live because liberty is there.

"If you have been likened unto the Lord Jesus Christ in His death, you shall be likened unto Him in your resurrection." (Romans 6:5)

Will such a liberty confine you and put you in slavery? Of course not, "for if the Son has made you free, then you are free indeed." (John 8:36)

And where did your liberty come from? This wonderful freedom, what is its source? You are free because you have His very own liberty!

It is at this point that true living begins. Nothing that God brings for the believer at this point will injure him gravely. What He asks of the believer will be much easier to accomplish than in times past. That is, there is so much less struggle, or none at all.

For instance, in the past the believer may have spent long hours in preparing to speak something or to teach something. He will eventually come to the point where there will be little preparation other than that which is done before the Lord. His heart and spirit will be so full that not as much preparation is needed. And the revelation is so much greater. The believer will have entered into that which the Lord told His disciples, "You will be given wisdom at that moment when the time comes to speak."

You can only come to such a place after the enduring of a great deal of weakness and experiencing a great deal of inability. The greater the loss, the greater will be the freedom.

Remember that a child of God simply cannot put himself in this place by his own efforts. If God does not prepare the circumstances and endow him with riches of His own life, the believer *cannot* possibly achieve these ends. Except by Him, he would not even desire them!

As you come to live in this experience of liberty and in this death and resurrection, you will find it very difficult to do many works you did before; and those you do will have to be done in a different way. This is not something to try to reason out. Simply know that your Lord has begun to do His work in you. His work will be the natural expression of what comes out of you. Not only will the source be different, but your view of what the Lord's work is will be changed. There will be a broader, fuller understanding of what "the work of God" is. What men see the work of God to be, through their own eyes, and what one sees the work of God to be when he looks through God's eyes are very different.

As to good works, these become a sort of "second nature"—God's nature—in you. When you hear someone speaking many words of humility, you notice that *you* are not humble. *You* cannot make *yourself* humble. If you tried, in your own strength, you would be rebuked for your faithlessness. Realize that being *dead* is a *lower* place than being *humble*. In order to be humble, you must first have been something. There is nothing lower than death; what is already dead is nothing, and there is nothing lower than nothing.

The pilgrim who has come to this place in his life is usually unknown, as very few of them have attained notoriety in their community or in their nation or in the world. This person is helped by being unknown because it allows him to preserve his rest in Christ. Remaining unknown helps one live in peace. This does not mean that all who know the Lord in this way remain unknown—not so—but most are.

There is a joy as well as an anonymity in this life. The joy is there almost imperceptibly. The joy is there primarily because fear is not there, driving desires are not there, and cravings for things have largely gone.

The Lord will enlarge such person's spiritual capacity beyond any given bounds.

Along life's way, you will meet or hear of people who are esteemed for their spiritual estate because of great ecstasies, swoonings, rapture, or their powers and gifts.

But let us look at this one who faints because he is so overcome spiritually. Is that a strength or a weakness? God draws that person away to be lost in Him, and yet that person faints? He is not strong enough to encounter and endure this drawing into God.

So when we speak of a great joy, we speak of things that go beyond raptures and visions. This is a joy that is constant as a *state* rather than *as an experience.*

What a glorious end!

Could the believer possibly have realized, when he lay in the dust of death and the horrors of the experience of dying, that such a life waited out there for him? If, while you were in the state of dying or being forsaken or seemingly forsaken, anyone had told you that such a glorious day would come, you would not have believed their words. Then learn this lesson: It is good to trust in God.

"Whoever puts his confidence in the Lord will not be put to shame." Romans 10:11

Can you see, dear one, how important it is to abandon yourself to God? Think how much suffering you would avoid if you simply continually yielded unto Him.

16

Most of the people who know the Lord Jesus Christ will not abandon their lives wholly to Him and trust in Him *alone*. And many who do say they are abandoning are abandoning in name only. Perhaps most believers really wish to abandon themselves to God, but only in *one* area. They reserve the right to have other areas all to themselves. Yet others wish to make a deal with God, to put limits on how far they will abandon themselves to Him. Finally, there are those who are willing to give themselves up wholly to God . . . but only on their own terms.

Then you must ask this question: Is this abandonment? True abandonment holds back nothing. Not life, nor death, nor salvation, nor heaven, nor hell. *Nothing.* Then throw your-self into the hands of God. Nothing but good can come from it. Walk assuredly on this stormy sea with the words of Christ to support you. Your Lord has promised to take care of all those who forsake themselves and abandon themselves to Him alone.

And if along the way you sink, as did Peter, realize it's because of your little faith. Boldly plunge ahead; meet all dangers that stand before you, not by effort but by faith. What are you afraid of, fearful heart? Are you afraid of losing yourself? Consider how little you are worth in your present condition. Consider this: Would the loss that you suffer really be all that great? You *will* lose yourself; that is, you will lose yourself if you are bold enough to abandon yourself to God. But remember that your life will be lost *in* Him. How wonderful a loss that is!

Why is it that we do not hear this preached? Why is it that everything else except this *is* preached? Many of those who call themselves Christians consider the things that we have discussed here to be madness. Or they will say that it is unbalanced. To the great minds of the Christian faith, these matters are some-thing that are just simply too low. People such as these must always feel that they are stable; they must feel that they are in control and that they are very balanced human beings. Yes, there is an extravagance in abandonment. This is something that they will not experience for they see themselves as too wise and mature.

When you submit to being annihilated, a great prize will ultimately be revealed to you; but you must be willing to be thrown around by your Lord like a leaf in a storm. In such moments offer no resistance. Fear not what the world says. To enter this place, you have to lose your reputation for being in control and your reputation for being a balanced individual. Be willing to be laughed at. Be willing to be rejected by those who set the standards of what a church member ought to be and what a Christian ought to be.

Today there are many who say that they want to have a good testimony in the eyes of men of this world. They say, "In this way God will be glorified." But this is not what they usually mean. What they are saying is they wish to have glory come to themselves.

To be really willing to be nothing in God's eyes (and also nothing in the eyes of men) and to continue having that desire in you when you are standing on the brink of the abyss of despair . . . this is something that is not common.

Do we dare go further? Can we speak of one

who has matured in his walk of abandonment to God? He will be someone not easily shaken by trials. There will be those who will shake him, even those whom God Himself chooses to put in his path in order that he be shaken. And as he reflects back on those times when he was unyielding to his God, those will be moments that will bring him pangs and a sense of deep, inner pain. But now, to resist the Lord would be much more difficult. And though he may resist the Lord, he probably will not be able to do so for very long. Why? Because there is a force at work in him. What that force is, he cannot say and he cannot understand; it is simply there.

The nature of God's dealing with any believer cannot easily be understood. His dealings are perfect, and your Lord will not leave one stone unturned when He begins to accomplish His purpose in your life. He arranges and uses every situation that comes into your life so that you will be His and so that, eventually, His work in you will be complete.

His ultimate goal in the maturing of a believer is to bring him to a point where he has lost everything—until there is no one in heaven nor on earth (except God alone) who can destroy him. There is no such thing as bondage to hold that believer; he is lost in God.

He still sees his spiritual nakedness, and yet he is clothed in purity. When a believer has tasted such a deep death, he no longer has the desire to go his own way. The death he has experienced was death indeed.

When one is dead, he can no longer be of himself. But be clear: A believer who is matured in the experience of abandonment is not beyond doing wrong. He is more aware of inner weaknesses than others. Yet he knows the strength of God within him even better than he knows his weakness. And this deep understanding brings to him a steadfastness. That steadfastness cannot be shaken by the world or hell or anything else.

Imagine that two people are living underneath the same roof and yet they are strangers to one another. They are near one another but they do not know each other. There is something of this truth in the life of the one who has matured over a long period of time. He is in the world, and yet he is a stranger to it. It is as though he lives somewhere else.

Do not think, though, that he is beyond suffering. Not at all. Probably he will experience more suffering than others. His relationship with that suffering will be quite different. There will be pain, there will be suffering in the flesh, and there will still be the cross. Nonetheless, there will be great joy in the spirit.

That joy will not *prevent* the suffering. Quiet joy is simply there in the *midst* of suffering.

The question is no longer, "Does this come from God?" All things (except sin) are God to such a one.

The items in the room are nothing of themselves. But if all the furniture is taken out of the room, then what the beholder would see would be nothing but the room itself. Now look upon your God in the same way. All creatures in heaven and earth seem to disappear and vanish. Yes, they are there, it is true. But they are separate from the believer. And they are not God. Nor are they any part of God Himself. But as the believer looks about him, even though the people are present and the circumstances are present, he views not the furniture but the room. Everywhere he looks the believer simply sees his Lord. His hand and the circumstances that come from His hand seem to blend into one. He has removed the furniture of this one's life, or at least He has made it unimportant to him.

As this believer walks in a continuing state of emptying himself, then his own experience becomes the experience of his Lord. Problems, trials, self-consciousness and suffering seem to disappear in God. Sorting out the good things and the bad things that are happening to him simply is irrelevant. This is something he will not do. He has come to rest in the circumstances of life because he has seen God in all of those circumstances.

If the whole world rises up against such a one and tells him that he is wrong, there will be a quiet peace within him that testifies otherwise. Now that may cause others to view him as being stubborn and obstinate, but he is not being obstinate. The truth lies here: He is no longer concerned about himself and his reputation.

Just what is this state of abandonment? A place where one sees only God. He is lost in God with Jesus Christ. This is as Paul expressed it. He has become one with his Lord, just as the river has become one with the sea. The river ebbs and flows with the sea, for the river no longer has a choice. The river has no strength to fight against the sea. Its will and the will of the sea have become united.

The boundless sea has absorbed the river and its limited waters. Now the river shares in all that the sea has. The sea carries the river along; the river cannot carry itself along. The river has become one with the sea. No, the river does not have all the qualities of the sea, but it is, nonetheless, in the sea.

This does not mean that this believer has lost his unique personality. No, never! It simply means that he is united with his Lord.

Yes, he can still be separated from his Lord, but that would be difficult to do unless it was God's choice for it to happen.

We earlier spoke of liberty. The man-made liberty is gone, but the liberty found in God alone continues. God is free. His liberty is not limited, nor is it confined in any way. This believer has become so free that he is hardly tied to this earth. He is free even to do nothing! And there is virtually no condition to which this believer cannot adapt himself.

What can one fear when found here! He has already experienced the loss of everything and he has already experienced death. Paul summed it up:

"Who shall separate us from the love of God? We are confident that neither death, nor life, nor principalities nor powers shall be able to separate us." (Romans 8:35-36)

Have you ever experienced a sense of confidence about something? You will recall that all doubt was excluded. Then, dear one, where is your confidence now? Can you not plant your confidence in the infallibility of God Himself?

The letters of Paul described the whole process of one's inward spiritual journey. The beginning of the journey, the progress of the journey, and the end of the journey. The world does not understand these things. But the believer, who has begun to experience these things, begins to understand them. If you are one who finds it so hard to give up everything to God . . . if you could only experience one moment of this deep inner life in God! You will discover the way there to be extremely difficult. But one day in this place of rest is worth years of suffering.

And how can your God lead you to this place? Whatever His ways are, they will be quite opposite to what you imagine. You see, your Lord builds by tearing down and He gives life by taking life away.

Neither space nor time matters when you glimpse the eternal realm. Everything around is as it should be; all places are good. Should God lead this one to the remotest parts of the earth, it will be just as it was in his own backyard. When the believer has experienced the fullness for which he was created, there really is nothing else to look for. All is God and all else is put away.

Your prayer life is God Himself. He *is* this "prayer" within you, incessant and uninterrupted. And as to sensing the presence of God, it is such a deep sensing that it is as though there were no sense there at all. Deep within you, though, there will be a constance of spirit.

The sense of His presence or the lack of the sense of His presence is now irrelevant to your life.

Whether you live or die, it is to the Lord. Never be concerned whether you live on earth or go to be with your Lord. Allow yourself to be transformed into the image of the One you love the most.

17

Do nothing. Remain still. Follow, without resistance, the impression that God imprints upon you. Be sure to remember that because you are not perfect, you are sure to make mistakes. Even as you begin to return to your spirit, and there learn to be led by God, you are still not infallible. So be careful (and humble yourself before God) so that you will not go astray.

Set aside all reflection, for you will find it hard to reason about how God leads you. If you are determined to pursue reasoning you may become very good at it and convince yourself to follow your own way. Or worse, you will *reason* that you are following God.

If you turn toward yourself and put all your

trust in yourself, you will experience the hell that befell Lucifer. He loved himself and became a devil. If you have once seen the glory of God, then falling away from Him is all the more horrible. Do not fall in love with yourself, but love God instead.

God transforms you a little at a time. He causes your spirit to be continually enlarged. No wonder David said:

"God, how great is the goodness which you have laid up for those who fear and love You!" (Psalm 31:19)

Although David had come to know his own sinfulness, he had also come to know the incredible grace of God even more. You who come to such a place are also the ones who all too gladly give their lives to glorify God. Your only desire is to see God glorified. This is because God has transformed your nature, and you have come to share in His concerns.

SeedSowers

Christian Books Publishing House
PO Box 3317 ● 4003 N. Liberty St.
Jacksonville, FL 32206
SeedSowers.com

1-800- ACT BOOK
1-800-228-2665

NEW

	Author
I, Jeanne Guyon	James
The Jeanne Guyon Nobody Knows	Edwards
Here's How to Win Souls	Edwards

SPIRITUAL CLASSICS

Experiencing the Depths of Jesus Christ	Guyon
Practicing His Presence	Lawrence/Laubach
Spiritual Guide	Molinos
The Seeking Heart	Fenelon
Intimacy with Christ	Guyon
Song of Songs	Guyon
Final Steps in Christian Maturity	Guyon
Spiritual Torrents	Guyon
Union with God	Guyon

THREE CLASSICS BY ONE AUTHOR

A Tale of Three Kings	Edwards
The Divine Romance	Edwards
Prisoner in the Third Cell	Edwards

INTRODUCTION TO THE DEEPER CHRISTIAN LIFE

Living by the Highest Life	Edwards
Secret to the Christian Life	Edwards
Inward Journey	Edwards

THE CHRONICLES OF HEAVEN

The Beginning	Edwards
The Escape	Edwards
The Birth	Edwards
The Triumph	Edwards
The Return	Edwards

THE FIRST-CENTURY DIARIES

The Silas Diary	Edwards
The Titus Diary	Edwards
The Timothy Diary	Edwards
The Priscilla Diary	Edwards
The Gaius Diary	Edwards

DEVOTIONAL

100 Days in the Secret Place	*Edwards*
Living Close to God (When You're Not Good at It)	*Edwards*

COMFORT AND HEALING

Healing for Christians Who Have Been Crucified by Christians	*Edwards*
Letters to a Devastated Christian	*Edwards*
Dear Lillian	*Edwards*
Suffering	*Pradhan*

BOOKS ON CHURCH LIFE

Climb the Highest Mountain	*Edwards*
How to Meet in Homes	*Edwards*
The Organic Church vs the "New Testament Church"	*Edwards*
The Christian Woman Set Free	*Edwards*

OLD TESTAMENT

Guyon's Commentaries	*Guyon*
Genesis ● Exodus ● Leviticus-Numbers-Deuteronomy ● Judges ● Jeremiah	

NEW TESTAMENT

Story of My Life, as Told by Jesus Christ	*The Gospels*
Your Lord Is a Blue Collar Worker	*Edwards*
The Day I Was Crucified	*Edwards*
Revolution, The Story of the Early Church	*Edwards*
Revolutionary Bible Study	*Edwards*
Unleashing the Word of God	*Edwards*
Acts in First Person	*The Book of Acts*

CHURCH HISTORY

Torch of the Testimony	*Kennedy*
Going to Church in the First Century	*Banks*
Passing of the Torch	*Chen*
When the Church Was Led Only by Laymen	*Edwards*
When the Church Was Young	*Loosley*

BIOGRAPHIES

I, Jeanne Guyon	*James*
Prem Pradhan, Apostle to Nepal	*Pradhan*
The Jeanne Guyon Nobody Knows	*Edwards*

EVANGELISM

Here's How to Win Souls	*Edwards*

RADICAL LITERATURE

How Paul Trained Men	*Edwards*
Are We Really Being Biblical?	*Edwards*
God Is Looking for a Man for the 21st Century	*Edwards*
Americanization of Christianity	*Edwards*
Concerning Our Missions	*Nee*